MYSTERIES UNCOVERED

TRUE STORIES OF THE PARANORMAL
AND UNEXPLAINED

MYSTERIES UNCOVERED

TRUE STORIES OF THE PARANORMAL AND UNEXPLAINED

Written by

Emily G. Thompson

Cover image: Nordic Forest by Martin Öhlander

With thanks to Victoria Armstrong for editorial assistance.

First published in Great Britain in 2020 by
Dorling Kindersley Limited
DK, One Embassy Gardens, 8 Viaduct Gardens,
London SW11 7BW

Copyright © 2020 Dorling Kindersley Limited
A Penguin Random House company

10 9 8 7 6 5 4 3
003–321182–Aug/2020

A CIP catalogue record for this book is available from the British Library.
ISBN: 978-0-24146-051-1

Set in 10.5/15pt Bembo MT Pro
Typeset by Jouve (UK), Milton Keynes
Printed and bound in Great Britain by Clays Ltd, Elcograf S.p.A.

For the curious

www.dk.com

MIX
Paper from
responsible sources
FSC™ C018179

This book is made from
Forest Stewardship Council™
certified paper–one small
step in DK's commitment
to a sustainable future.

Contents

The Lost Colony of Roanoke

To this day, nobody knows what became of the 115 pioneering souls who made up the Roanoke Island Colony, America's first-ever English settlement. Were they killed? Did they succumb to disease or starvation? Did they leave the island for the nearby mainland? Speculation about their fate has endured for centuries. What became of the Lost Colony remains one of the US's greatest – and earliest – mysteries.

———————————

"The English were very backward in trying to manage in that environment."

Historian Karen Kupperman

———————————

The first Roanoke Island Colony was established in 1585. It was sponsored by the renowned explorer and polymath Sir Walter Raleigh, at the behest of Queen Elizabeth, who hoped the settlement would yield gold, silver, and other riches that could be brought back to England. Ralph Lane, governor of the colony, called the island, situated just off the coast of what is now North Carolina, "the goodliest and most pleasing territory of the world". The first group of 108 colonists built a fort and cabins, but after 11 months, they were forced to return to England owing to scarce food and deteriorating relations with the American Indians in the area. In fact, the party left so quickly that three men who had left the camp on an expedition were left behind. What became of this unfortunate trio remains a mystery.

Shortly after the colonists abandoned Roanoke Island, the sea captain Sir Richard Grenville arrived. Discovering the deserted settlement, he left behind some men and enough supplies for two years. These men also vanished.

Two years later, in July 1587, a second group of settlers, including 90 men, 17 women, and 11 children, was dispatched to found a permanent settlement in the New World. Sir Walter Raleigh had bankrolled a settlement for the shores of Chesapeake Bay. However, the captain dumped the colony at Roanoke Island instead. Some historians have speculated that the navigator, Simon Fernandes, wanted to drop the settlers off as quickly as possible so that he could return to sea to attack Spanish ships that were sailing up the coast, loaded with valuable cargo from Spain's South American colonies.

The settlers were led by John White, who was an artist and not an explorer. He brought along with him his pregnant daughter, Eleanor, and her husband, Ananias Dare. Eleanor gave birth to a daughter, Virginia – the first English child born in the New World – on 18 August.

Despite – or because of – the fact that virtually nothing is known about her, Virginia Dare's name has echoed through the centuries, with speculations concerning her mysterious fate sparking controversy. She became a symbol of innocence and purity; a legendary heroine of tales celebrating the first white settlers' pioneering spirit; her name was used to advertise all sorts of goods; and numerous places in North Carolina were named after her. To American Indians and African Americans, the name Virginia Dare would come to have a very different significance: It would become a potent symbol of white supremacy by Anglo-Americans seeking to reaffirm their racial dominance.[1]

Soon after Virginia's birth, White left the settlers on Roanoke Island while he sailed back to England for more supplies. He had anticipated the round trip to take months. Delayed by war between England and Spain, however, he did not return until 1590. When he finally landed on Roanoke, he discovered that the entire colony had vanished. His account of what he found there was published in 1600 by Richard Hakluyt in *Principal Navigations, Voyages and Discoveries of the English Nation*.

White recorded that there was no sign of a struggle or battle. In fact, there was little evidence of the settlement site at all, except for a few cannonballs and a log stockade that had enclosed the colonists' dwellings. There were intriguing clues, potentially hinting at their whereabouts, notably the word "Croatoan" carved into a post and "Cro" carved into a tree. Before White had left for England, the majority of the Roanoke Colony had been planning to move "50 miles into the maine", referring to the mainland.

Presuming that they had joined the friendly Croatan tribe that lived on Croatoan Island, White planned to sail there next day. However, a storm blew White and his fleet out to sea. The weather damaged White's ship, forcing the crew to abort the search and sail back to England, never to return.

White took solace in the apparent message that was carved into the post: "I greatly joyed that I had found a certain token of their being at Croatoan where Manteo was born." Manteo was a leader from Croatoan Island who became friendly with the Roanoke Colony and was even baptized a Christian on Roanoke Island. However, no Englishman would ever see the Roanoke colonists again.[2]

Numerous conspiracy theories and plausible scenarios have attempted to explain the settlers' disappearance. Historians, determined to fill in the blanks of history, have spent centuries examining the few tantalizing clues that hint at the possible fate of the "Lost Colony". Some commentators believe that the colonists resettled elsewhere, while others think they merged and interbred with American Indians.

There has also been widespread speculation that they were massacred by a local tribe. By the time the colonists settled on Roanoke Island, the area had been the scene of regular conflicts for generations. Not only were the region's tribes disrupted by European colonization; the Spanish had explored and settled along the East Coast for decades before the English arrived. Some American Indians, such as those in the Chesapeake area, were friendly; but other tribes, such as the Powhatan of coastal Virginia, who were led by a powerful chief named Wahunsonacock, were fiercely opposed to English settlers encroaching on their territory.

Around 17 years after the doomed attempt at colonization on Roanoke Island, explorers from the Jamestown Colony in Virginia – the first permanent English settlement in the New World – resolved to investigate what had happened to the Roanoke community. According to William Strachey, Secretary of the Jamestown Colony from 13 June 1610, to the summer of 1611, the Roanoke Colony had been murdered by the Powhatan. He described this incident as the "slaughter at Roanoke". Allegedly, the Roanoke Colony had moved north to the southern shores of Chesapeake Bay. The Chesapeake Indians were the only tribe in the area who had not submitted to Wahunsonacock's Powhatan and they accepted the Roanoke colonists as their allies.[3] Research showed that the Roanoke Colony would not have fared well without assistance from friendly natives. According to the historian Karen Kupperman, who specializes in 16th- and 17th-century colonialism, "The English were very backward in trying to manage in that environment."

By the time the Jamestown Colony was established, the Powhatan domain was vast, having expanded to about 30 sub-tribes.[4] Strachey reported that Wahunsonacock's Powhatan had wiped out the Chesapeake Indians – and presumably the Roanoke colonists with them – after his priests had warned him that "from the Chesapeake Bay a nation should arise, which should dissolve and give end to his empire".[5]

Strachey writes of this massacre in his account of the Jamestown

Colony titled *The Historie of Travaile into Virginia Britannia,* which, though written in 1612, was not published until 1849. Strachey also records the discovery, in two American Indian settlements, of two-storey houses with stone walls. This led him to speculate that some native people had learned building techniques from the Roanoke colonists – indicating that the settlers must have allied with the tribes at some point. The Jamestown Colony also received reports that some members of the Roanoke Colony had survived the massacre by the Powhatan. Strachey relates that he spoke with a friendly member of Powhatan's tribe named Machumps, who assured him that there were indeed survivors from the Roanoke colony, some of whom were being held by a chieftain named Gepanocon, who was now forcing them to forge copper into weapons and utensils. However, Jamestown search parties found no English-speaking people, and the community's focus quickly shifted towards its own survival. John Smith, a member of the Jamestown Colony, published his own report on the expedition titled *The Proceedings and Accidents of the English Colony in Virginia.* His report makes no mention of any mass slaughter in the area. Although some historians have since speculated that Smith did not want to deter potential future attempts at colonization, no archae-ological evidence exists to support claims of a massacre of the Roanoke colonists, nor is there legitimate evidence of its occur-rence in Powhatan tribal history.

Nevertheless, tension between local tribes forced out of trad-itional hunting grounds by English colonists, who brought with them deadly new weapons and even worse diseases, was clearly high. Several years after the Jamestown Colony investigation, the Powhatan attacked the Jamestown Colony, killing 347 people – a quarter of the entire population.

In 1937, a 9.5-kg (21-lb) rock was discovered in a swamp 96.5 km (60 miles) west of Roanoke Island on the Chowan River by a Californian tourist named L. E. Hammond. Carved into one side of the stone were the words:

> *"ANANIAS DARE & VIRGINIA*
> *WENT HENCE UNTO HEAVEN 1591*
> *ANYE ENGLISHMAN SHEW*
> *JOHN WHITE GOVR VIA"*

On the other side, the following message was carved:

> *"FATHER SOONE AFTER YOV*
> *GOE FOR ENGLANDE WEE CAM*
> *HITHER ONLIE MISARIE & WARRE*
> *TOW YEERE ABOVE HALFE DEADE ERE TOW*
> *YEERE MORE FROM SICKNES BEINE FOVRE &*
> *TWENTIE*
> *SALVAGE WITH MESSAGE OF SHIPP VNTO US*
> *SMAL SPACE OF TIME THEY AFFRITE OF REVENGE*
> *RANN*
> *AL AWAYE WEE BLEEVE YT NOTT YOV SOONE*
> *AFTER*
> *YE SALVAGES FAINE SPIRTS ANGRIE*
> *SVDDIANE*
> *MVRTHER AL SAVE SEAVEN MINE CHILDE*
> *ANANIAS TO SLAINE WTH MVCH MISARIE*
> *BVRIE AL NEERE FOVRE MYLES EASTE THIS*
> *RIVER*
> *VPPON SMAL HILL NAMES WRIT AL THER*

ON ROCKE PVTT THIS THEIR ALSOE SALVAGE
SHEW THIS VNTO YOV & HITHER WEE
PROMISE YOV TO GIVE GREATE
PLENTIE PRESENTS
EWD"

The letters "EWD" are thought to stand for "Eleanor White Dare", and the inscription is believed to be a message to her absent father, John White. The inscription suggests that Ananias and Virginia were massacred not long after White returned to Roanoke Island. They were buried on a hill near the river and their names carved into a second stone near their graves. This stone was the first of what would become known as the "Eleanor Dare Stones". Over the ensuing years, another 47 stones were uncovered, including some as far away as Georgia. The fundamental problem with the stones, however, was the question of authenticity. For example, one stone included the hyphenated names of several English families – such as Pole-Carew – even though hyphenated names were not in use before the end of the 18th century.[6] In 1941, the *Saturday Evening Post* dismissed the stones as a massive fraud in an article entitled, "Writ on Rocke".

However, a 2009 article by University of North Carolina Wilmington professor David La Vere published in the *North Carolina Historical Review* argues that the original stone could be authentic because it was the only one written in a style and prose consistent with Elizabethan English. An Elizabethan scholar La Vere asked to examine the language on the stone was "particularly interested in the word 'salvage' (for savage) which was used in English (from the Italian word for forest) during only a few years . . . The Lost Colony fits in with that period".[7] Experts have not been able to discredit

9

this stone, as they have the 47 additional stones. "If this stone is real, it's the most significant artefact in American history of early European settlement," said Ed Schrader, a geologist and President of Brenau University in Georgia, where the stone is kept. "And if it's not, it's one of the most magnificent forgeries of all time."[8]

In 1998, new research claimed that the Roanoke Colony had simply had monumental bad luck. The colonists had arrived during a time of severe drought, bringing starvation and death. Dennis Blanton, the director of the William and Mary Center for Archaeological Research, and a group of tree-ring specialists from the University of Arkansas, came to this conclusion by studying tree rings from ancient bald cypress trees along the coasts of Virginia and North Carolina. They gathered hints of weather conditions by measuring the width of tree rings from the trunk of these trees, which can live for over 1,000 years. They discovered that the rings were much smaller than average between 1587 and 1589 and between 1606 and 1612, the early years of the Jamestown settlement, indicating that growth had been much restricted in those years, possibly owing to lack of water. "The Roanoke and Jamestown Colonies have both been criticized for poor planning, poor support, and for a startling indifference to their own subsistence. But tree-ring reconstruction indicates that even the best-planned and supported colony would have been supremely challenged by the climatic conditions," wrote Blanton in his report.[9]

According to Matthew D. Therrell of the University of Arkansas, the years between 1587 and 1589 marked the most extreme drought of any comparable period during the entire 800 years of the tree-ring record. While there was no weather data available from the time, the researchers said that the tree-ring data was similar to the short-term drought that was recorded from the 1940s in the same area. This led to speculation that the settlers died or were forced to move elsewhere.

Modern archaeological investigations have been similarly inconclusive. In fact, it isn't even known exactly where the Roanoke colonists originally settled on Roanoke Island. Much of the search for the Lost Colony has focused on earth berms shaped like an old English fortification at the north end of Roanoke Island, where Fort Raleigh Natural Historic Site now stands. The National Park Service reconstructed these mounds in the 1950s, and numerous archaeological digs have been conducted here. A number of artefacts found during the digs indicate that the area served as a workshop for scientist Thomas Harriot and metallurgist Joachim Gans, who were part of the first Raleigh-sponsored expedition that returned to England in 1586. However, none of these items suggested that the Lost Colony was ever located there. "We have looked and we have looked and we have looked. The main settlement is not here. It is someplace else," said Guy Prentice, who oversees excavations for the National Park Service Southeast Archaeological Center.[10]

In 2012, a 16th-century map of Virginia and North Carolina drawn by then-governor John White was examined by experts in the British Museum at the request of the First Colony Foundation. Using advanced imaging techniques, they uncovered hidden markings drawn with invisible ink. The drawings appeared to show a "fort-like image" in what is now Bertie County, North Carolina. The Roanoke colonists could have resettled here after abandoning their original camp. For the next three years, archaeologists excavated a 79-square-metre (850-sq-ft) rural site south of the Chowan River bridge, near Edenton, North Carolina, around 80.5 km (50 miles) from Roanoke Island. The area – which became known as Site X – had been inhabited for centuries, first by American Indians, and then early English settlers, before becoming the site of a governor's plantation. Here, archaeologists discovered a number of Elizabethan artefacts, including bale seals used to verify cloth quality, 16th-century nails, firing pans from snaphance firearms, and pieces of pottery jars for storing dried and salted fish.[11]

Alastair Macdonald, officer and archaeologist for the First Colony Foundation, commented: "Elizabethan artefacts appear on very few other sites in Carolina at all. There's virtually none . . . the concentrations of Elizabethan objects are on Roanoke Island, the site of the Croatoan village [on what is now Hatteras Island, off the coast of North Carolina], and our site . . . No other English or Europeans were in that area until Nathaniel Batts came in the 1650s. It is interesting, too, that there were artefacts from several pots, it wasn't just one object that was broken. That suggests there might have been a certain continuity at the site for a period of time."[12]

As mentioned earlier in this chapter, on finally returning to the original Roanoke settlement, John White reported that the word "Croatoan" had been carved on a post and the word "Cro" on a tree, possibly suggesting that the colonists had relocated to nearby Croatoan (now Hatteras) Island. Over the years, ancient fragments dating back to Elizabethan times have been found on Hatteras Island. In 1993, Hurricane Emily unearthed hundreds of artefacts. These caught the attention of Professor of Anthropology David Phelps of East Carolina University. Throughout the 1990s, he conducted digs on the island and uncovered evidence of native and English assimilation.[13] However, the origin of the Elizabethan artefacts remains uncertain, and shipwrecks could account for at least some. Furthermore, Croatan Island was visited by English mariners on a number of occasions between 1585 and 1587 who sometimes remained there for several weeks. In addition, there was an English presence on the island throughout the 17th century.

In 1998, Phelps' group discovered a small gold ring with a lion motif buried on Hatteras Island. This ring was linked to the Kendall family of Devon and Cornwall. A Master Kendall allegedly participated in the first colonization attempt in 1585. However, this seeming breakthrough was scotched in 2017 when archaeologist Charles Ewen ordered the ring be tested at East Carolina University with an X-ray fluorescence device, which revealed that the object was brass, not gold. Ewen speculated that the ring had probably been brought over by European settlers and traded to American Indians long after the Roanoke Colony vanished. "Everyone wants [the ring] to be something that a Lost Colonist dropped in the sand," Ewen remarked to *Smithsonian* magazine.[14]

While the evidence is still speculative, many believe that the original Roanoke colonists joined an American Indian tribe. "Something happened between 1587 and 1590, we know they were there in 1587 and we know they were gone in 1590, and it is certainly expected that some of them went to the village of Croatoan, but we think that area would not have been large enough to support all of the villagers," observed the First Colony Foundation's Alastair Macdonald.[15] Fred Willard, director of the Lost Colony Center for Science and Research, hypothesized that after White left for England, the Roanoke colonists became hungry and fearful of the increasingly hostile American Indians and realized that they needed to relocate if they wanted to survive. Seeking safety in numbers, they merged with the friendly Croatan tribe.[16]

Although the Roanoke Colony vanished in 1590, it wasn't actually considered "lost" until almost 250 years later. Its disappearance was an obscure, largely forgotten event until 1837, when an article in

The Ladies' Companion written by Eliza Lanesford Crushing coined the term "the Lost Colony". Contemporary Elizabethans would not have considered the fate of the settlers particularly mysterious. They would have come to the conclusion that the settlers simply abandoned the colony, joined a local tribe, adopted their ways, and intermarried to survive. "If I were hungry, and knew John White might never return with supplies, I would start practising my Algonquian and learning Indian methods for hunting, fishing, and farming," said Andrew Lawler, author of *The Secret Token: Myth, Obsession, and the Search for the Lost Colony of Roanoke*.[17]

A 1608 Virginia Company's pamphlet titled "A True and Sincere Declaration" certainly suggests that the Roanoke Colony intermingled with a native tribe. An extract from it explains, "Some of our nation, planted by Sir Walter Ralegh [sic], are yet alive, within fifty miles of our fort." The Jamestown colonists may even have come close to finding them, until their search was thwarted by the warlike Powhatan tribes. The pamphlet adds, "Though denied by the savages speech with them, they found crosses and letters, the characters and assured testimonies of Christians cut in the barks of trees."

A later search party was told that there were "four men clothed" who had originally come from the Roanoke Colony; however, this expedition was halted shortly afterward, without further inquiries for survivors being conducted.

In 1701, a naturalist named John Lawson was visiting Hatteras Island when American Indians from the coast told him that "several of their ancestors were white people and could talk in a book (read), as we do; the truth of which is confirmed by grey eyes being found frequently among these Indians, and no others".[18] Towards the latter part of the 19th century, it was noted that a number of

American Indians in the south eastern part of North Carolina were light-skinned with pale eyes, and many had surnames matching those of the Roanoke colonists. In 1885, these individuals were officially recognized by the state as Croatan Indians. Lawson speculated that members of the Roanoke Colony had assimilated with the Croatan Indians after they lost hope of White returning from England.

While this theory has been accepted, both by 16th-century and 21st-century historians, according to author Andrew Lawler, this idea was "so repellent to white Americans in the 19th and 20th centuries, that they made the colonists' disappearance a mystery, rather than as a first step toward the multicultural nation that we increasingly are becoming."

The mystery of the Lost Colony has intrigued historians and the popular imagination for centuries. It has become part of American folklore and, just like Bigfoot or the Loch Ness Monster, the colonists and their fate have proved elusive, their trails evaporating into nothingness. After all this time, nobody has yet been able to pinpoint exactly where the Roanoke Colony built their fort or houses. No artefacts have been found that can definitely be linked back to them. Some believe that the settlement has been covered or even washed away by the waters of Roanoke Sound. Others believe that the Lost Colony will be lost forever, and that this might not be such a bad thing: "It will help keep the mystery alive," said Noel Hume, retired chief archaeologist at Colonial Williamsburg. "Things that get solved tend to go away."

The Mystery of the *Mary Celeste*

In the winter of 1872, the American merchant ship *Mary Celeste* was discovered drifting, abandoned, yet still seaworthy – a "ghost ship", inviting comparisons with the mythical tale of the *Flying Dutchman*. The fate of the *Mary Celeste*'s ten-man crew, somehow lost in the vast Atlantic Ocean, remains one of the greatest of all maritime mysteries. Were they murdered? Kidnapped by pirates? Spirited away by some supernatural force? Or were they simply the tragic victims of bad luck and human error?

"She brought disaster on every man that put his trust in her."

James Franklin Briggs, the nephew of
Captain Briggs of the *Mary Celeste*

---

1 8 May 1861, was a good day for the shipyards of Spencer's Island, situated some 125 km (78 miles) northwest of Halifax, Nova Scotia, Canada: it saw the launch of the *Amazon*, a 30.5-m (100-ft), two-masted brigantine. Unfortunately, the omens for the *Amazon*'s future were not good – her captain, Robert McClellan took sick and died of pneumonia on her maiden voyage, within just 48 hours of taking command. Shortly afterwards, the ship collided with a fishing boat off the coast of Maine and received a deep gash in her side. The *Amazon* was subsequently damaged on several occasions, finally running aground during a storm in Cow Bay, Cape Breton Island, in 1867.

Badly damaged, the *Amazon* was bought by a dealer named Alexander McBean, from Glace Bay, Cape Breton Island. He sold the brig to an American merchant named Richard W. Haines, who undertook repairs. Maritime lore decrees that it is bad luck to change the name of a ship, but after spending the sizable sum of $8,000 on repairs – not much less than the ship was worth – Haines did just that, renaming her the *Mary Celeste*. Haines' choice of name was allegedly inspired by Maria Celeste, the illegitimate daughter of Galileo and Marina Gamba, Galileo's mistress.

19

Haines' motives for restoring the wrecked ship remain obscure. A December 1872 article in the *Boston Globe* cited that Haines "knowingly and fraudulently obtained a certificate of register for said brig", so he may well have seen some (possibly shady) money-making possibilities in his investment.

In 1869 the craft was seized by Haines' creditors and taken on by a reputable New York shipping firm, James H. Winchester & Co., which hired her out to small firms. The *Mary Celeste* also underwent a major refit that added a deck and increased her gross tonnage by 50 percent. Cabins were moved between decks, and several other alterations were made to her structure.

On 7 November 1872, the *Mary Celeste* set sail from New York City, under the command of Captain Benjamin Spooner Briggs, an experienced seaman who owned one third of her. She was bound for Genoa, Italy, with a cargo of 1,701 barrels of denatured alcohol, a poisonous type of ethanol used for fortifying wine. Captain Briggs was accompanied on the voyage by his wife, Sarah, and their two-year-old daughter, Sophia, as well as a seasoned crew of seven men: Albert G. Richardson, first mate; Andrew Gilling, second mate; Edward William Head, steward and cook; Volkert Lorenzen, seaman; Boz Lorenzen, seaman; Adrian Martens, seaman; and Gottlieb Goodschadd, seaman.[1]

"Our vessel is in beautiful trim and I hope we shall have a fine passage but I have never been in her before and I can't say how she'll sail. We seem to have a very good mate and steward and I hope I shall have a pleasant voyage," wrote Captain Briggs in a letter to his mother before departure. Sarah echoed this sentiment in a letter to her mother-in-law: "Benji thinks we have got a pretty peaceable set this time all around if they continue as they have begun. Can't tell you how smart they are."[2]

All appeared well until 4 December, when the British brig *Dei Gratia* spotted the *Mary Celeste* adrift around 740 km (400 nautical miles) off the Azores. Shortly before setting sail, Captain Briggs had met Captain David Morehouse of the *Dei Gratia* and they had chatted about their upcoming voyages. The *Dei Gratia* was also bound for the Mediterranean, leaving just a few days ahead of the *Mary Celeste*. When Captain Morehouse spotted the *Mary Celeste* near the Azores, he knew the ship immediately. He also noticed that something was amiss. She appeared to be floundering aimlessly with the wind. He noted that the *Mary Celeste* "was under very short canvas steering very wild and evidently in distress".[3] It was clear to the captain that no one was at the wheel. Two of her sails had been blown away and another was flapping in the wind; however, there was no distress signal.

Captain Morehouse drew his ship level with the *Mary Celeste* and hailed her. Receiving no response, he saw that the small yawl that served as the ship's lifeboat was missing from the stern davits. The deck was eerily empty and there was nobody at the helm. Crewmen from the *Dei Gratia* boarded the drifting ship and found that everything was neat and in order. The only sound was the eerie creaking of the ship's timbers. They wondered if some sort of plague had overcome the *Mary Celeste*'s crew and they would be discovered below decks. However, they soon realized that the ship was completely deserted. There was no sign of the crew or of Captain Briggs and his family. There was no evidence of any kind of struggle and nothing seemed amiss.

The *Mary Celeste* had just sailed into maritime history.

A search of the ship failed to uncover any clues as to the crew's whereabouts. The cargo was still on board, as well as the crew's personal belongings and six months' worth of food rations. In the captain's cabin, Briggs' watch was hanging from a lamp bracket above the table. A half-drunk cup of coffee sat by the captain's writing station, where he meticulously recorded the ship's daily activities and observations. The last entry had been made at 6 am on 25 November. It recorded the weather conditions and noted that the ship was 11 km (6 nautical miles) off the Azores. Beside the logbook was the beginning of a letter that read:

"Fanny, my dear wife,"

The words appeared to be the beginning of a letter written by the first mate, Albert G. Richardson, to his wife, which had been abruptly interrupted. Also found in the captain's cabin was a piece of cloth on Sarah Briggs' sewing machine, indicating that she had been sewing when she was disturbed. "There seemed to be everything left behind in the cabin as if left in a hurry, but everything in its place. [We] noticed the impression on the Captain's bed as of a child having lain there," read the crew of the *Dei Gratia*'s report. The hull, mast, and yard goods were in good condition, as was the deckhouse, and the captain's cabin. The only things that were missing – other than the lifeboat – was the captain's chronometer, sextant, and navigation book, along with the ship's register and various other documents.[4]

There appeared to be no reason for abandoning the ship, and there was no evidence that the *Mary Celeste* had encountered unusually bad weather or been involved in an accident. The *Dei Gratia*'s crew did discover that there was around 1 m (3 ft 6 in) of water in the ship's hold; however, this posed no significant danger and the ship was still seaworthy. The search party concluded that – for whatever reason – the *Mary Celeste*'s crew must have abandoned ship in a great hurry, for they had left behind their pipes and tobacco – something they felt no sailor would purposely do.

A skeleton crew from the *Dei Gratia* sailed the *Mary Celeste* to Gibraltar, some 1,930 km (1,200 miles) away. The new crew managed to pump out the water in the hold in a few hours and the ship was declared fit enough to sail "around the world with a good crew and good sails".

Once the *Mary Celeste* reached Gibraltar, the crewmen applied for a salvage payment. British officials examined the ship and convened a salvage hearing, which was usually limited to determining whether the salvagers were entitled to payment from the ship's insurers. Captain Morehouse estimated that he would be able to claim about $17,400 on the ship and about $18,000 for the cargo.

The man in charge of the inquiry was the Attorney General of Gibraltar, Frederick Solly-Flood, QC. He suspected that foul play was involved and launched an inquiry, ordering a survey of the ship on 23 December 1872. He obstinately stuck to his belief that some sort of conspiracy was being perpetrated, even insisting that the missing Captain Briggs had plotted with Captain Morehouse to share the salvage rights of the *Mary Celeste*. However, the court found no evidence that anything was untoward. No bodies had been discovered and nothing had been stolen from the ship.

"I am of the opinion that she was abandoned by the master and crew in a moment of panic and for no sufficient reason," stated Captain R. W. Shufeldt of the US Navy, after inspecting the ship. "I reject the idea of a mutiny from the fact there is no evidence of violence about the decks or cabins."[5] In a letter to the US State Department, Horatio Sprague, the American Consul to Gibraltar, wrote: "This case of the *Mary Celeste* is startling, since it appears to be one of those mysteries which no human ingenuity can recreate sufficiently to account for the abandonment of this vessel, and the disappearance of her master, family, and crew, about whom, nothing has ever transpired."

Eventually, the salvagers – the crew from the *Dei Gratia* – received a payment of roughly one-sixth of the $46,000 for which the *Mary Celeste* and its cargo had been insured. This was poor compensation for the trouble that the salvagers had gone to, and indicative of a cloud of suspicion that lingered over the ship's disappearance and the involvement of the *Dei Gratia*'s crew.[6]

For a while, friends and family of the *Mary Celeste*'s crew clung to hopes that they would be found. The Secretary of the US Navy requested that all vessels passing in the vicinity of the *Mary Celeste*'s location should heave to for 24 hours to search for survivors; however, attempts to find clues as to the fate of the crew proved fruitless.

Following the Gibraltar hearing, the *Mary Celeste* was released to her part-owner, James H. Winchester, and returned to service. On 25 February, a fresh crew arrived on board to deliver the ship's cargo of alcohol to its scheduled destination, Genoa.

The *Mary Celeste* once more sailed the seas – presumably uneventfully – for a further 12 years, before meeting a sad end in 1885. Her captain, Gilman Parker, had loaded her with a cargo of cheap rubber boots and cat food, before deliberately running her aground on Rochelais reef, Haiti. He then filed an extortionate insurance claim for an expensive cargo that didn't exist.[7] Three months after his trial, Gilman Parker died in obscure circumstances. His first mate died three months later. One of the plotters of the insurance scam committed suicide, and all the firms involved in the fraud went bankrupt.[8]

Sailors are famously superstitious and often attribute accidents at sea to unknown evils lurking below the surface. Many believed that the *Mary Celeste* was jinxed. According to James Franklin Briggs, Captain Briggs' nephew, the *Mary Celeste* should have been named "Mary Diablesse", or "Mary the She-Devil", because "she brought disaster on every man that put his trust in her".[9]

The Briggs family as a whole seems to have been dogged by appalling bad luck. Several of Captain Briggs' siblings had tragic ends. His oldest brother, Nathan Henry, died at sea years before the *Mary Celeste* made her mark on history. His youngest brother, Zenas Marston, succumbed to yellow fever while in port at Beaufort, North Carolina, shortly before Captain Briggs' own disappearance. Another brother, Oliver Briggs, was lost at sea when his brig, the *Julia Hallock*, foundered in the Bay of Biscay. Captain Briggs' sister, Maria, drowned at sea with her husband, Captain Joseph Gibbs. His father, Nathan Briggs, also a sea captain, died after being struck by lightning outside his home, Rose Cottage, in Sippican Village, Massachusetts.

Another theory, popular in the latter part of the 19th century, was that the crew had drunk the industrial-strength alcohol onboard and committed mutiny. It was also posited that alcohol vapours from the cargo had expanded in the Azores heat and blown off the main hatch, prompting the crew to fear an imminent explosion. The chief mate of the *Dei Gratia*, Olivier Deveau, claimed that the head of one of the alcohol barrels had been blown off. However, the rest of the *Dei Gratia* crew reported that the main hatch to the cargo hold was secure and they did not smell any alcohol. Furthermore, if alcohol fumes had caused an explosion, the ship would have gone up in flames, yet there was no evidence of fire.

Around the time of the original inquiry into the *Mary Celeste* case presided over by Gibraltar's suspicious Attorney General

Solly- Flood, whispers of foul play made their way into newspapers. According to a February 1873 article in the *Indianapolis News*, Captain Briggs was "murdered off the Bay of Biscay by his crew, who mutinied, and also killed his wife and child".[10]

This hypothesis was vigorously asserted by Fanny Richardson, the first mate's wife: "I always believed and always will believe that my husband, Captain Briggs, Mrs Briggs, her baby, and the cook were murdered by the crew . . . I think it is far more likely that the crew broke [the cargo] open, drank it, lost their heads, then murdered the four Americans on board and got away in the after boat and were lost."[11]

Nine of the 1,701 barrels of alcohol in the hold were indeed empty; however, these empty ones were recorded as being made of red oak, not white oak, like the rest. Red oak is known to be more porous than white, and therefore more likely to leak. Furthermore, if the crew had drunk poisonous raw alcohol from the cargo, it would have blinded or soon killed them.

This theory that the crew had lost their heads and mutinied was based on simple prejudice – the majority of the crew were foreign. Among the doomed members, German brothers Volkert and Boye Lorenzen became suspects owing to the fact that none of their personal belongings could be found on the abandoned ship. According to a descendant, however, the brothers had lost their personal items in a shipwreck earlier in the year.

One of the more unusual items found on board was a sword with reddish stains on it; reddish stains were also noted on the deck. Attorney General Solly-Flood deduced that these stains were blood. According to Captain Briggs' family, the sword had been picked up by the Captain while touring a battlefield at Fiume, Austria. However, this was contradicted by Fanny Richardson, who said that the sword was a trick sword belonging to her husband. Later, a British naval physician, Dr J. Patron, proved that the so-called bloodstains on the sword and deck were nothing more than rust spots and fragments of a vegetable substance.[12] "From the preceding negative experiments I feel myself authorized to conclude that according to our present scientifical knowledge there is no blood in the stains observed on the deck of the *Mary Celeste* or on those found on the blade of the sword I have examined," he reported.

The mystery of the *Mary Celeste* might well have drifted into obscurity if a young Sir Arthur Conan Doyle, the future creator of Sherlock Holmes, had not published a short story inspired by the incident titled "J. Habakuk Jephson's Statement" in the January 1884 edition of *Cornhill Magazine*.

In Doyle's tale, the ship, fictionalized as the *Marie Celeste,* is in perfect order – with no water in the hold – when discovered by the *Dei Gratia*. Doyle's *Marie Celeste* also has all her boats present and intact – whereas one boat was missing from the real *Mary Celeste*. Other dramatic touches, such as the *Dei Gratia*'s crew finding breakfast served but uneaten, helped fire the imaginations of readers, who took his story to be true.

Doyle's eponymous narrator is an American doctor and well-known Abolitionist who served with the Union army during the American Civil War. The doctor takes a sea voyage for his health aboard the *Marie Celeste* – described as a "snug little ship" – but the peaceful trip goes awry when the captain's wife and child disappear, presumably swept overboard, and the grief-stricken captain shoots himself in the head. The boat is later boarded by a group of spear-carrying warriors, party to the murderous vengeance of one of the passengers, a former slave bent on revenge. The ship's crew are thrown overboard, but the narrator is spared and cast adrift in a canoe because he carries a black stone – a powerful good-luck token – previously given to him by an elderly freed slave for championing the liberation of African Americans.

Doyle's sensationalistic tale gave rise to numerous theories about the real fate of the *Mary Celeste*'s crew, ranging from the comparatively mundane – insurance fraud – to a freak natural disaster, piracy, murder, and even attack by a giant sea monster. The *Mary Celeste* mystery also helped establish the legend of the Bermuda Triangle – the notorious area famed for the unaccountable disappearances of ships and, later, aircraft – despite the fact she hadn't sailed near those waters.

Speculation concerning an attack by a monster of the deep is easy to dismiss because the ship had sustained no serious damage. Piracy is also unlikely because the ship was still full of cargo and the crew's personal items, including money, were untouched. "Acts of God" explanations have included a seaquake or a waterspout.

Perhaps the most plausible scenario stems from the discovery of a sounding rod – a tool used to test the depth of water – on the *Mary Celeste*'s deck, along with the disassembled components of a pump used to empty water from the hold. On its preceding voyage, the *Mary Celeste* had carried a cargo of coal, and the ship had just recently been refitted. Coal dust and construction debris might have fouled the pump, which could explain why it had been taken apart. With the pump inoperative, Captain Briggs would not have known how much water was actually in the hold. Perhaps Captain Briggs grew so concerned about the water in the hold that he convinced himself that the *Mary Celeste* could sink at any moment and ordered the ship to be abandoned. However, Captain Briggs was an experienced sailor and widely respected for his seamanship. He wasn't prone to panic or hysteria. "There was never a question that he would do something irrational," commented Ann MacGregor, writer of a 2007 television documentary *The True Story of the Mary Celeste*. In all likelihood, if Captain Briggs did order the ship to be abandoned, he must have been within sight of land. According to his last record, they were only 9.6 km (6 miles) off the Azores. He might have decided that they were close enough to land to deploy their lifeboat – with, as it turned out, disastrous consequences.

The mystery of the *Mary Celeste* is by no means unique in maritime history. Over the decades, numerous ships have been found drifting in the ocean with not a crewman aboard. However, in those cases, the crew eventually reached safety or their fate was easily established by evidence left on board. On that fateful December day in 1872, the *Mary Celeste* sailed forever into international maritime legend, a silent witness to tragedy. Her story captured the world's imagination, perhaps because it provided the New World with one of its earliest and most absorbing nautical legends. The mystery of the *Mary Celeste* – a fruitful source for writers, maritime sleuths, and TV documentarists – continues to resonate into the 21st century.

The Flannan Lighthouse Mystery

The Flannan Isles are wild, treacherous, and desolate – little more than jagged rocks, clawing out of the fierce Atlantic Ocean. No wonder they are known locally as "The Seven Hunters". Perched precariously on the highest point of Eilean Mòr, the largest of the islands, is Flannan Isles Lighthouse. In the year 1900, this eerie building became the centre of one of Scotland's most celebrated and enduring mysteries when three lighthouse keepers – James Ducat, Thomas Marshall, and Donald McArthur – inexplicably vanished into thin air.

"I was left on the island alone for three hours . . .
You could really feel the ghosts . . . I found it a very
frightening and sinister place. It is almost
caught – or lost – in time."

The composer Peter Maxwell Davies

The Flannan Isles lie approximately 32 km (20 miles) west of Lewis, the largest island of Scotland's Western Isles. To the west, the bleak Atlantic Ocean stretches endlessly. Consisting of seven islands, the isles are sometimes referred to as "the other country" by shepherds from Lewis who winter their sheep there. The area around the isles is one of the most exposed in the UK. Waves may be as high as 15 m (50 ft), sometimes up to 30 m (100 ft).

The sea around the isles is particularly dangerous to navigate, and after several shipping disasters, during the 19th century a lighthouse was built to warn passing ships. Flannan Isles Lighthouse was built on the highest point of Eilean Mòr, which is little more than a large rock in the middle of the ocean, around 550 m (600 yds) long by 183 m (200 yds) wide. "The task of constructing it was both laborious and dangerous. The sea was seldom really calm and it was necessary to blast landing places out of the solid rock, to erect cranes, and to hoist all the materials required to the top of the cliff," wrote John Gilbert Lockhart in his 1929 book *Strange Adventures of the Sea.*

After four years of difficult work, the lighthouse was completed in 1899. It was built of stone to resist the Atlantic gales. It was

23 m (76 ft) high, and installed at the top was a 140,000-candlepower lamp, visible for a distance of 44. 5 km (24 nautical miles). There were two landing places, one to the east and one to the west, to be used according to wind direction. The lighthouse had four keepers in total: James Ducat, Thomas Marshall, Donald McArthur, and Joseph Moore. However, at any one time, one would be on shore. The reason behind this was because it was feared that one lighthouse keeper could go mad, two lighthouse keepers might kill each other, but three lighthouse keepers would keep a dynamic going for a long time in isolation.[1]

This reasoning had a solid basis in past experience: in 1801, tragedy had befallen two keepers, Thomas Howell and Thomas Griffith, at the Smalls Lighthouse, 40 km (25 miles) off the coast of Pembrokeshire, Wales. Griffith died following an accident, and Howell was left to fend for himself alone with the decomposing corpse. The two men were well known for their fierce arguments, so Griffith was fearful of disposing of the body by throwing it into the sea, believing he would be accused of murder. He constructed a makeshift coffin, which he secured to a rail outside the light-house. The wild weather tore it open, and Griffith's decomposing arm flapped against the lighthouse window. Freak storms prevented a relief ship from reaching the lighthouse for weeks, by which time Howell's mental and physical sufferings had caused him to lose his mind.

The Flannan Lighthouse keepers' duties were to trim the wicks, oil the machinery, and keep the tower in repair between visits of the supply ship. Each man spent six weeks on the lighthouse and then two weeks off, leaving three keepers to man it. Every 20 days, depending on weather conditions, the relief ship, *Hesperus*, arrived from Oban – the nearest port on the Scottish mainland – to take one man off and deposit his replacement, along with any provisions the keepers required. During his two weeks on the mainland, the keeper would reside at the township of Breasclete, on the north side of Loch Roag, where cottages had been built for the men and their families.[2]

James Ducat had been reluctant to go to the Flannan Isles but was persuaded to take the role of keeper by Northern Lighthouse Board (NLB) superintendent Robert Muirhead. In 1990, Ducat's daughter Anna remembered, "[My father] said it was too dangerous, that he had a wife and four children depending on him, but Mr Muirhead persuaded him because he had such faith in him as a good and reliable keeper." Anna recalled the day her father left well, for it was ingrained in her memory forever: "It was a lovely sunny day and my brother Arthur and I were playing in the high-walled gardens. My father came out of the house and picked each of us up in his arms and gave us a hug and a kiss, then he walked very quickly away up the road. We ran after him shouting, 'Daddy, Daddy', and he stopped at the road end and waited for us, picked each of us up again, and gave us another kiss. I have always wondered if he had some kind of premonition that he would never see us again."[3]

The first sign that something was amiss at the lighthouse was shortly after midnight on 16 December 1900. Captain Holman of the steamer *Archtor* was passing the islands when he noticed that there was no light coming from the lighthouse. He radioed: "No beacon flashed from the Flannan Lighthouse, northwest of Cape Wrath." He also reported back to the NLB about the lighthouse's missing beam. The reason for this would not emerge for ten days.

On 26 December, the relief ship *Hesperus* arrived at Eilean Mòr with fresh provisions, as well as Christmas cards and gifts from the keepers' loved ones back on shore. The boat had been delayed six days by a perilous storm that had battered the coast of Scotland. As the *Hesperus* approached the barren rock, the crew noticed that the flagstaff had no flag, the usual provision boxes had not been left on the landing stage for restocking, and none of the lighthouse keepers were there to welcome them ashore. In a bid to alert the keepers, the *Hesperus* blew its whistle and fired a rocket, which exploded high in the winter air. Still no one appeared.[4]

Captain Harvie launched a boat carrying the relieving keeper, Joseph Moore, to the island. It put in at Eilean Mòr's east landing. In a letter to the NLB, Moore recalled, "I was the first to land, leaving Mr McCormack and his men in the boat till I should return from the lighthouse." Moore climbed apprehensively up the 160 steps to the lighthouse station. The entrance gate and outside doors were closed and the lighthouse was deserted. Inside, Moore saw that the clock had stopped, the beds were all neatly made, and despite the severe weather, the fire clearly had not been lit for some days. Gravely concerned, Moore returned to the *Hesperus* and related his findings. Two other men came ashore to help him search the island for the three keepers. However, no trace of them could be found.

Captain Harvie sent a telegram to the mainland that was forwarded to the NLB. It read:

"A dreadful accident has happened at Flannans. The three keepers, Ducat, Marshall, and the occasional have disappeared from the island.

"On our arrival there this afternoon no sign of life was to be seen on the Island. Fired a rocket but, as no response was made, managed to land Moore, who went up to the Station but found no Keepers there. The clocks were stopped and other signs indicated that the

accident must have happened about a week ago. Poor fellows they must been blown over the cliffs or drowned trying to secure a crane or something like that.

"Night coming on, we could not wait to make something as to their fate. I have left Moore, MacDonald, Buoymaster, and two Seamen on the island to keep the light burning until you make other arrangements. Will not return to Oban until I hear from you. I have repeated this wire to Muirhead in case you are not at home. I will remain at the telegraph office tonight until it closes, if you wish to wire me."

The searchers discovered the daily record slate. The last entry was made at 8 am on Saturday, 15 December. Presumably, the men had vanished shortly after that time. Saturday morning's work at the lighthouse and in the living quarters had been completed. The big lamps had been trimmed, ready to be lit, and the oil fountains and canteens were full. According to the official reports, in the kitchen, everything was tidy and the dishes had been washed and put away. However, according to other reports, a meal of salted mutton and boiled potatoes lay half eaten on the table, and a chair was toppled over on the floor. Some rumours also alleged that the door to the lighthouse was locked and that Moore had a key.[5]

While investigating the lighthouse, the searchers discovered that Ducat's and Marshall's sea boots and oilskins – which would typically be worn outside in rough weather – were missing. However, McArthur's oilskin was still hanging on its peg. The rules of light-house keeping were that only two men were allowed outside the lighthouse at any one time, while one remained inside to watch over the lamp. This led to speculation that Ducat and Marshall had ventured outside while McArthur had remained inside. The sailors from the *Hesperus* then searched down by the east landing, where they had disembarked on the island. Finding nothing amiss, they made their way to the west landing. Here they found evidence of damage, probably caused by strong winds. The lighthouse keepers had a wooden box containing ropes, crane handles, and other bits and pieces that they kept secured in a crevice in the rocks. This box was nowhere to be found, and the searchers supposed that it had been washed away by the tides. An iron railing that ran around the platform had been ripped out and broken in several places. A large rock had fallen from the top of the cliff down onto the path.

According to contemporary reports, the weather logs had been updated daily by Ducat up until 12 December, when Marshall seemingly took over. However, these logs have never been verified and mysteriously disappeared, leading some to suspect some kind of cover-up. The logs allegedly read:

December 12th

Gale N. by NW. Sea lashed to a fur. Never seen such a storm. Waves very high. Tearing at the lighthouse. Everything ship-shape. James Ducat irritable. Storm is still raging, wind steady. Storm-bound. Cannot go out. Ship passing and sounding foghorn. Could see the cabin lights. Ducat quiet Donald McArthur crying.

December 13th

Storm continued through the night. Wind shifted W by N. Ducat quiet. McArthur praying.

There was no entry for 14 December, but there was an undated entry that was presumably from the following day:

Noon. Grey daylight. Me, Ducat, and McArthur praying. 1 p.m. Storm ended. Sea calm. God is over all.[6]

According to Moore, his companions were not the praying kind, unless they were awfully afraid. He didn't think that a storm would scare them enough to warrant crying and praying. The searchers concluded that, after being confined to the lighthouse for several days, when the storm finally abated, they went to the west landing to see what damage it had caused. But what about McArthur? Did he venture outside without his wet-weather gear? And if so, why? "At this point we reach the crux of the mystery," wrote John Gilbert Lockhart. "The men are at the landing place. What disaster can overtake them there on a comparatively calm day?"

That question has never been answered, and the men's disappearance has never been fully explained. Over the past century, there have been fantastic tales of madness and murder as well as bizarre theories involving malevolent ghostly figures, violent seabirds, pirates, and even sea monsters.

For years, fishermen have sworn that they have heard the cries of shipwrecked seamen on the Flannan Isles, calling out in the dead of night for help, but when they try to seek them out, they find nobody. According to local legend, ghostly figures have been seen standing on the rocky shore with the waves crashing around them, beckoning passing ships. But when the ships get closer, the figures disappear.[7] John Milne, the acting principal in charge of Flannan Isles Lighthouse after the men vanished, later said that there was a "heavy presence" on the island and that on several occasions, he had turned around – expecting to see somebody there – but nobody ever was. He also claimed that he heard voices echoing in the night and somebody calling out the missing keepers' names.

Local legend also says that on the night of 15 December, two sailors in a small boat called the *Fair Wind* spotted an ominous-looking longboat carrying a number of men passing their boat near the Flannan Isles. The crew said that they hailed the boat, but received no response. They also claimed that the boat appeared eerily pale and the sight of it chilled them to the bone.[8]

Even today, many people have felt a strange presence on the Flannan Isles, and some have even refused to set foot on them. The composer Sir Peter Maxwell Davies, who wrote an opera, *The Lighthouse*, based on the mystery, recalled, "I was taken out by a helicopter by the Northern Lighthouse Board – and I was left on the island alone for three hours. It was incredibly creepy and spooky. You could really feel the ghosts. I kept walking up and down those steps from which the men must have met their fate. I found it a very frightening and sinister place. It is almost caught – or lost – in time."[9]

Superstitious folk place a lot of credence on the legend of the Phantom of the Seven Hunters – a mysterious, shadowy figure with some connection to St Flannan, a 6th-century Irish bishop who built a chapel on Eilean Mòr. According to local legend, the Phantom of the Seven Hunters was infuriated by the intrusion onto his island by the lighthouse and keepers. Their disappearance was his retribution.

The mystery of the three missing lighthouse keepers was not the only tragedy connected to the Flannan Islands. In previous years, a keeper had fallen to his death from the lantern gallery and four men had drowned when their boat had overturned while trying to approach one of the landing stages.[10]

Then there are – of course – more straightforward conclusions. NLB superintendent Robert Muirhead, who had known the missing keepers well, was saddened and baffled by their disappearance. He wrote, "The Board has lost two of its most efficient keepers [Ducat and Marshall] and a competent Occasional [McArthur]."[11] Muirhead had visited the Flannan Isles Lighthouse just a week before the keepers were thought to have vanished. He recalled that he had "the melancholy recollection that I was the last person to shake hands with them and bid them adieu". His report concluded: "I am of opinion that the most likely explanation of the disappearance of the men is they had all gone down on the afternoon of Saturday, 15 December, to the proximity of the west landing . . . and that an unexpectedly large roller had come up on the island, and a large body of water going up higher than where they were and coming down carried them away with resistless force."

Six months earlier, the lighthouse keepers had been fined three shillings by the commissioners because improperly secured landing tackle at the west landing had been damaged during a storm. Perhaps, when severe weather lashed the island that December, the keepers feared that similar damage might occur again. When the storm died down, Ducat and Marshall could have gone down to the west landing to investigate and make any necessary repairs, leaving the "Occasional", McArthur, alone in the lighthouse. McArthur, a local man, might have known about a freak wave pattern that occurs in the gully under the west landing stage after strong storms. This can suddenly send a massive swell crashing up the cliff face, like a tidal wave, taking everything in its path. While sitting in the lighthouse alone, perhaps it dawned on him that his colleagues were in grave danger and he ran out in just his shirt to warn them, only to be swept away with them by sudden powerful waves.

According to Donald Macaulay, a descendant of McArthur, this is the most likely scenario. "I am certain the three keepers on Flannan were caught in an ocean swell which had created a huge wave that swept them away," he said.[12] Alasdair Macaulay, a reporter with BBC Radio, researched the keepers' disappearance and came to the same conclusion. While investigating the incident, he heard about a nearby woman who was hanging her washing out to dry on 15 December when she spotted a massive wall of water coming in from the west. She managed to run back inside her home before the wave reached the shore. It hit with such force that her washing line and her washing were swept away. John Love, author of *A Natural History of Lighthouses,* wrote, "For me, and many others, including lightkeepers themselves, there is no mystery and never has been. There is no need to invoke the sinister or the paranormal, it was purely a tragic act of nature – the men got swept away in the storm by abnormally rough seas."[13]

However, this seemingly logical conclusion has not convinced everyone. Some commentators have pondered why three experienced keepers – Ducat had 22 years as a lighthouse keeper behind him – would venture out in extreme weather. If the weather was bad enough for rough tides, surely they would have stayed indoors, knowing the dangers all too well. Rumours attempting to explain the men's disappearance are still rife. Among the more sensational is that one of the keepers killed his two colleagues and threw their bodies over a cliff. Overcome with remorse, the murderous keeper then committed suicide by launching himself into the ocean.

Keith McCloskey, author of *The Lighthouse: The Mystery of the Eilean Mòr Lighthouse Keepers*, is unconvinced that the keepers were swept away by a large wave. Muirhead's report cited that the keepers had gone out after lunch. However, according to McCloskey, outside jobs were always conducted in the morning, particularly in winter when there were fewer hours of daylight. "The afternoons were used for rest. I got all the weather records from the meteorological office and there were prevailing winds coming from the west and a gale building up that would have been hitting the west landing. So for them to have gone out there so late in the afternoon seems a bit strange." While researching the mystery, McCloskey spoke to several lighthouse keepers, who said that, when the weather was bad, they just stayed indoors and shut up shop.

McCloskey also interviewed descendants of Donald McArthur, who confirmed that he was not a full-time lighthouse keeper and that he was only on Eilean Mòr because one of the other keepers, William Ross, had been taken ill and was on extended sick leave. "When you're stuck on a rock with two other people for that long, you can imagine tempers starting to fray. I worked on the theory that there may have been violence involved, which is how I finished the book."

Dr John Hay, a doctor in Uig on Lewis for 24 years, is of the same opinion as McCloskey. Hay's wife's uncle, Donald Macleod, was also a lighthouse keeper and had known Ducat, Marshall, and McArthur. "Uncle Donald said one of the men was known to be unstable and morose. He may have been unhappy during the meal and a struggle broke out. He could have killed both the other men and then killed himself or the fight carried to outside the lighthouse and they were all lost over the cliff. But Uncle Donald was sure a struggle was the initial cause," he suggested.[14]

The mysterious disappearance of the Flannan Lighthouse keepers inspired the 2018 movie *The Vanishing* and was also referenced in 2019's *The Lighthouse*. In addition, *The Lighthouse*, an opera by Peter Maxwell Davies, books, songs, and poems have ensured that the tragedy has never been forgotten. One of the most affecting memorials is "Flannan Isle", a 1912 poem by William Gibson, written from the point of view of three men from the *Hesperus* who find the lighthouse deserted. It contains these lines:

> *"We seemed to stand for an endless while,*
> *Though still no word was said,*
> *Three men alive on Flannan Isle,*
> *Who thought, on three men dead."*

The Disappearance of Amelia Earhart

Pioneering aviator Amelia Earhart was a world-renowned figure and trailblazing female role model. Intrepid, free-spirited, and ambitious, she was famously the first woman to fly solo across the Atlantic. There seemed to be almost nothing she could not accomplish in her chosen field – including the longest-ever round-the-world flight. She set out to make history. Instead, she flew into legend.

———————

"Please know I am quite aware of the hazards. I want to do it – because I want to do it. Women must try to do things as men have tried. When they fail, their failure must be but a challenge to others."

Amelia Earhart

———————

Aviator Amelia Earhart and her navigator Fred Noonan have been missing for more than eight decades. On 2 July 1937, they – and their aeroplane – vanished without trace, just short of completing Amelia's greatest achievement to date: circumnavigating the globe around the equator. Two years later, the United States government declared that their plane had crashed in the Pacific Ocean, killing them both on impact. However, their bodies have never been found. The mystery of their fate has inspired books, documentaries, TV shows, movies, songs, and even museums.

Amelia Earhart was born on 24 July 1897, in Atchison, a city tucked away in the northeast corner of Kansas, around 90 km (55 miles) from Kansas City. Atchison is a quaint city often known as "Little Switzerland" owing to its rolling hills and valleys.[1] The area is dotted with beautifully restored Victorian mansions and a trolley car, originating back to the Old Santa Fe Train Depot, that meanders through charming homes and historic sites. It was here on a bluff overlooking the Missouri River that, as a young woman, Amelia first felt the lure of the skies.

Amelia's parents, Edwin and Amy, struggled financially, but always provided for Amelia and her younger sister, Muriel. When

Amelia was about seven years old, the Earhart family visited the 1904 St Louis World's Fair. There Amelia experienced her first-ever rollercoaster ride. Overjoyed by the sensation of speed and excitement, she decided to build her very own rollercoaster in the backyard. It consisted simply of a wooden box that flew across wooden planks that had been greased with oil.[2]

When the pressures of providing for the family became too much for him, Edwin turned to alcohol. He closed the doors of his failing law office and took up employment at the Rock Island Railroad in Des Moines, Iowa. The plan was for Edwin and Amy to get settled in Iowa and find a place for the family to live. Until then, Amelia and Muriel would be staying with their grandparents in Atchison, where they enjoyed a secure upper-middle-class lifestyle, attending private school and frequently visiting the local library. At Christmas, Edwin and Amy would return to Atchison with gifts for their girls, including sleds and rifles, which at the time were almost exclusively gifts for boys. When Amelia was 11 years old, she and Muriel left Atchison to be with their parents in Des Moines, but often returned to their grandparents for long visits. In 1915, Amy and Edwin separated and Amelia attended six different high schools before finally graduating from Chicago's Hyde Park High School.

As a young woman, Amelia developed a strong independent streak. She was convinced that women were just as capable as men in many areas that were traditionally considered "men's work". She firmly rejected the traditional roles society seemed to have reserved for women and collected magazine and newspaper clippings about inspirational women who had established themselves in positions that were typically held by men. She took work with the Red Cross as a nurse's aide in the Spadina Military Hospital in Toronto during World War II, and briefly studied medicine at Columbia University. When Amelia turned 21, her father paid $10 for her to take a ride in an aeroplane during an air show in Long Beach, California. From that day forward, Amelia knew that her life's ambition was to fly. She saved the $500 needed for aviation lessons, taking a number of small jobs, including as a photographer, truck driver, clerk, and stenographer.

As Amelia was nurturing her love for flying, women were taking the aviation industry by storm. Blanche Scott was the first American woman to pilot an airplane in 1910, and in 1912 she became the first woman to fly the English Channel. In 1911, Harriet Quimby became the first woman to earn a pilot's licence. On the day that Harriet died in 1912, Ruth Law flew her very first solo flight, and the following year she became the first woman to loop the loop. Amelia was greatly inspired by these pioneering women, but their achievements were continually overshadowed by those of male aviation heroes, such as Eddie Rickenbacker, Howard Hughes, and Charles Lindbergh, who dominated the media in the 1920s.

From the moment she took the controls, Amelia had her eyes set on the record books. Her impetuousness was evident when, after less than three hours of flying lessons, she spent all her savings on a yellow Kinner Airster biplane that she called *Canary*.

In May 1923, Amelia became the sixteenth American woman to obtain a pilot's licence; the same year, she took her first shot at an aviation record, becoming the first woman to fly higher than 14,000 feet. Following this feat, she continued to log time in *Canary* until she sold it in 1924.

While retaining her aviation dreams, Amelia's strong desire to make a contribution to society led her to become a social worker at Denison House in Boston. She commuted there in style, behind the wheel of her yellow Kissel Speedster automobile. Denison House was a women-run institution that provided support to local residents, particularly the many new immigrants to Boston's South Cove neighbourhood. Amelia threw herself into the work with typical enthusiasm. Her considerable personal drive soon led to her organizing adult education programs, women's clubs, and coaching girls' basketball and fencing. She also put her flying skills to good use – in 1927, she dropped leaflets advertising a Denison House fundraiser over Boston and nearby Cambridge.

However, the following year would bring Amelia worldwide fame. In June, piloting a tri-motor Fokker F7 named *Friendship* with a small crew onboard, she became the first woman to fly across the Atlantic Ocean. When she landed in Burry Port, Wales, she had accomplished a goal that three women had died trying to accomplish that very year. People were inspired by her bravery and news of her feat spread across the world. On her return to the US, she was met with a grand parade. The following year, she became the first woman to fly solo across the United States in both directions.[3]

Amelia bettered these considerable achievements on 22 May 1932, by becoming the first woman to fly the Atlantic Ocean solo. She set out from Harbor Grace, Newfoundland, Canada, bound for Paris, France. All she brought with her was a toothbrush, a container of hot soup, an ice pack, and straws for three cans of tomato juice.

Owing to ice forming on the wings and mechanical issues, Amelia had to cut her flight short, landing in a field in Derry, Northern Ireland. Despite this, she had set a transatlantic speed record of 14 hours and 56 minutes. She followed this feat in January 1935, by becoming the first person to fly the Pacific solo, when she flew from Honolulu, Hawaii, to Oakland, California.

Amelia took to her newfound fame gracefully. She earned herself the nickname "Lady Lindy", after her male aviation counterpart, Charles Lindbergh, although this was a name she wasn't fond of. An inspiration to women everywhere, she hoped that her work and accomplishments would inspire other women to pursue their dreams. In 1931, she married the publishing heir George Palmer Putnam, but only on the understanding that she would lose none of her independence. In a 1935 parade in her hometown of Atchison, she told the crowd, "It is my fondest hope that women will become more interested, as pilots or passengers, or last but not least, let their men fly. Women have been labelled the greatest sales resistance in flying. They won't go up and they won't let their men go up. If mother says father will stay down, father stays down." In Washington, she became the first woman to be awarded the Distinguished Flying Cross and National Geographic Society medals. "Her success expanded the powers of women, as well as men, to their ever-widening limits," said President Herbert Hoover.[4]

The one feat left for Amelia to accomplish was a round-the-world flight and, in early 1935, this is what she set her sights on. "To me it can be, if successful, a happy adventure," she said of her next challenge. "And perhaps there is a place in this prosaic world for the right kind of adventuring." On her 38th birthday, the airplane she had selected for her global flight was delivered: a twin-engine Lockheed Electra monoplane. For the next five months, the aircraft was prepared with all the equipment needed to tackle the almost 48,280-km (30,000-mile) route around the world.

In January 1937, Amelia was ready to embark on her latest adventure. She would be assisted by navigator Fred Noonan, who was well-known in aviation circles, having worked as chief navigator for Pan American Airways. They set off from San Diego and arrived in Honolulu in a record-breaking time of 16 hours. From there, they had planned to fly more than 3,220km (2,000 miles) to Howland Island, a tiny speck of an island in the Pacific, and from Howland to the city of Lae in Papua New Guinea. However, as they attempted take-off, the Lockheed Electra crashed. Uninjured, Amelia and Fred shipped the aircraft back to California for repairs, and in five months' time they were ready to attempt the round-the-world trip once again. Due to different wind patterns in the summer months, they decided to reverse their route and fly in an easterly direction, circling the world at the Equator.

On 2 July 1937, Amelia and Fred took off in their heavily loaded Lockheed Electra from Lae, Papua New Guinea. They were carrying 5,000 litres (1,100 gallons) of fuel for the 18-hour flight to Howland Island, where they planned to land for refuelling. It was the heaviest amount of fuel that they had ever carried, and the small aircraft was 50 percent overloaded. It was not even 10 am, but the blazing tropical sun was already beating down as they slowly rose above the Huon Gulf, skimming so close to the sea that water sprayed the wings. They had already flown 32,187 km (20,000 miles) in the previous six weeks, and now only 11,265 km (7,000 miles) of Pacific Ocean separated them from their destination of California, from where they had commenced their momentous journey. Once they landed, Amelia would be the first woman to have flown around the world.

Unbeknown to the group of eager well-wishers who had gathered at Lae airfield that morning to wave Amelia and Fred goodbye, they would be the last people to ever see them.

Amelia had arranged a schedule with the airways radio operator at Lae, Harry Balfour. She was to transmit messages at 18 minutes past each hour and then Harry was to transmit his messages at 20 minutes past each hour. At 10:20 am, 11:20 am, and 12:20 pm local time, Harry informed Amelia of strong headwinds, but received no response. The stronger the headwind, the faster an aircraft must fly, and the faster an aircraft must fly, the more fuel it burns. At 2:18 pm, Harry finally received a radio transmission from Amelia. She said, "Height 7,000 feet, speed 140 knots." She then said "Everything okay." At 3:18 pm local time, Amelia reported, "Position 4.33 south, 159.7 east – height 8,000 feet over cumulus clouds – wind 23 knots." This meant that Amelia and Fred were still on course for Howland Island. They had stuck to their original route, but if excessive fuel consumption continued, they would arrive at Howland Island with little to no fuel remaining.[5]

Amelia and Fred now had to decide whether to continue the flight or turn back. Darkness was fast approaching, and if they turned around, they risked crashing into the mountainous peaks of Bougainville Island between their location and Lae, which was also surrounded by mountains over 3,657 m (12,000 ft) high. With the aeroplane being overweight, if they lost an engine, it would be highly unlikely that they could maintain sufficient altitude to clear the mountains. Furthermore, by the time they approached Lae, it would be too dark and dangerous to attempt to manoeuvre around the mountains. They thus resolved to push on to Howland Island. As they approached the Gilbert Islands, they transmitted a message to this effect. At this point, they were roughly four hours away from Howland Island.

At 6:15 pm GCT, Amelia transmitted to the USCGC *Itasca*, a picket ship stationed at Howland Island to provide air navigation and radio links to Amelia as she came in to land. She said, "Please take bearing on us and report in half hour. I will make noise in microphone – about 100 miles out." She listened back for a reply but heard nothing other than noise and static, meaning that either the *Itasca* was not transmitting or her receiver was not receiving its signals. They continued en route and began their descent toward Howland Island at 6:33 pm GCT. Fred had estimated it should take them ten minutes to arrive, but ten minutes passed and Howland Island was not yet in sight. Amelia transmitted once again, stating, "KHAQQ calling *Itasca* we must be on you but cannot see you, but gas is running low been unable to reach you by radio. We are flying at altitude 1,000 feet." There was no reply. Moments later, Amelia informed the *Itasca* that they were circling back, believing that they had missed Howland Island. "We are on the line of position 157 dash 337. Will repeat this message. We will repeat this message on 6210KC. Wait listening on 6210. We are running north and south."

After broadcasting this transmission, Amelia and Fred vanished from the skies forever.

Amelia was evidently aware of the dangers. She had written a letter to be released to the media if she were lost at sea: "Please know I am quite aware of the hazards. I want to do it – because I want to do it. Women must try to do things as men have tried. When they fail, their failure must be but a challenge to others."

As soon as it became apparent that Amelia Earhart had vanished, the US Navy put out an "all ships, all stations" bulletin. The authorities asked anybody with a radio to listen in to the frequencies that Amelia had been using on her flight: 3105 and 6210 kHz. President Franklin Roosevelt ordered a massive search, which involved planes from the aircraft carrier USS *Lexington* and flying boats from the battleship USS *Colorado*.

Amelia's disappearance sparked the largest and most expensive air and sea search in American history, but to no avail. Amelia's husband, George, subsequently embarked on his own search. Before the doomed flight, Amelia had written him a note: "I know that if I fail or if I am lost you will be blamed for allowing me to leave on this trip; the backers of the flight will be blamed and everyone connected with it. But it's my responsibility and mine alone."[6] Two years after their disappearance, the US government officially declared Amelia Earhart and Fred Noonan dead *in absentia*.

Since their disappearance, theories have abounded from a number of competing researchers and internet sleuths who have dedicated much time, energy, and resources to one of aviation's most perplexing mysteries.

In 2017, a black and white photograph surfaced that lent weight to the theory that Amelia and Fred had somehow survived. The photograph, which was aired on the History channel's documentary *Amelia Earhart: The Lost Evidence*, depicted a group of people on a dock and, in the background, a woman with her back to the camera. Some have suggested that the woman in the photograph could be Amelia, and that another figure facing the camera may be Fred. The photograph is believed to have been taken on a dock on Jaluit Atoll in the then-Japanese-held Marshall Islands in 1937. It was discovered by a retired federal agent in 2012 in the National Archives in College Park, Maryland.

"The hairline is the most distinctive characteristic. It's a very sharp receding hairline. The nose is very prominent. It's my feeling that this is very convincing evidence that this is probably Noonan," said Kent Gibson, a forensic analyst who has studied the photograph. "When you pull out, and when you see the analysis that's been done, I think it leaves no doubt to the viewers that that's Amelia Earhart and Fred Noonan," agreed Shawn Henry, a former FBI executive director. According to retired government investigator Les Kinney, the image "clearly indicates that Earhart was captured by the

Japanese". However, the Japanese authorities claimed that they had no record of her ever being in custody.[7]

This wasn't the first time that such a supposition had been put forward. The Marshall Islands theory had been around since the 1960s, when residents claimed that they had witnessed the aircraft land and seen Amelia and Fred in Japanese custody. In fact, so much weight was placed on this theory that trained dogs were sent to the island by The International Group for Historic Aircraft Recovery (TIGHAR) and the National Geographic Society to search for traces of Amelia. TIGHAR researchers came away from the island stating that there was no evidence she was ever there and that the woman in the photograph had hair that was much longer than Amelia's.

Despite TIGHAR's findings, it is this explanation for Amelia and Fred's disappearance that Mike Campbell, author of *Amelia Earhart: The Truth at Last*, believes is the most plausible. Campbell stated that years of research led him to believe that Amelia and Fred were captured by the Japanese after being mistaken for American spies. According to the retired journalist, "*Amelia Earhart: The Truth at Last* dismantles and debunks the popular theories that Amelia's Electra crashed and sank off Howland Island on 2 July 1937, or landed at Gardner Island, now Nikumaroro, where the suddenly helpless fliers died of starvation on an island teeming with food sources."[8]

This theory divided the internet when it surfaced once again in 2017, garnering mixed reactions around the globe. Campbell's claim was discredited by Tokyo-based military blogger Yota Yamano, who discovered the same image in the archives of the National Diet Library, the national library of Japan. The photograph formed part of a Japanese travelogue published in Palau in October 1935, two years before Amelia vanished.[9]

One of the most popular theories remains that Amelia and Fred landed near Nikumaroro Island, which is located in the Pacific Ocean, around 4,180 km (2,600 miles) north of New Zealand.

On 23 September 1940, a British party was exploring Kiribati's Nikumaroro Island for habitation when British colonial officer Gerald Gallagher discovered buried human remains, including a skull and 13 other bones. D. W. Hoodless, a British doctor at the Central Medical School in Suva, Fiji, examined them and declared that they were those of a short and stocky man. The remains were quietly forgotten about before disappearing. Then in 1991, a fragment of aluminium patch was discovered in Nikumaroro by TIGHAR. According to TIGHAR, this fragment matched an aluminium patch that was unique to Amelia's Lockheed Electra. At the beginning of her trip, the custom-made window had been removed from her aircraft and replaced by a modified patch. "Its dimensions, proportions, and pattern of rivets were dictated by the hole to be covered and the structure of the aircraft. The patch was as unique to her particular aircraft as a fingerprint is to an individual," read a statement on TIGHAR's Earhart Project site.[10] Shortly thereafter, the researchers on Nikumaroro Island stumbled across fragments of an old shoe, which they suggested was a size 9 woman's blucher oxford from the mid-1930s with a recently replaced heel and glass eyelets. Photographs of Amelia taken around ten days before her disappearance show her wearing similar shoes.

With this new discovery, TIGHAR began to focus heavily on Nikumaroro Island. In 1998, they announced that they had discovered the original British files on the earlier human remains that had been found on the island. These files recorded measurements of the human remains. According to forensic anthropologists

Karen Burns and Richard Jantz, the shape of the bones "appears consistent with a female of Amelia's height and ethnic origin".[11]

Almost a decade later, TIGHAR visited Nikumaroro Island once again. This time, they were assisted by four border collies – trained sniffer dogs. The dogs were all drawn to the same area underneath a tree, leading TIGHAR to believe that Amelia and Fred had died at this spot 80 years earlier. In 2018, the human bones discovered on the island were re-examined by Richard Jantz from the University of Tennessee. He stated that, although it was originally believed that they belonged to a man, forensic osteology was not well developed in the early 20th century. Employing the computer program Fordisc – used by forensic anthropologists to compare estimates of bone lengths – he declared that the remains were those of a woman. His findings, published in the journal *Forensic Anthropology*, concluded that "the only documented person to whom they may belong is Amelia Earhart".[12]

The same year, TIGHAR declared that they had collected testimony from dozens of people who had allegedly heard broadcasts of Amelia and Fred pleading for help in the days after their disappearance. Testimony spanned from St Petersburg, Florida, to Toronto, Canada. A teenage girl in St Petersburg heard the desperate pleas: "Water's high, water's knee deep – let me out," and "Help us quick. A Toronto housewife heard this highly disturbing cry: "We have taken in water . . . we can't hold on much longer."

This is what TIGHAR's research revealed: "Scattered across North America and unknown to each other, each listener was astonished to suddenly hear Amelia Earhart pleading for help. They alerted family members, local authorities, or local newspapers. Some were investigated by government authorities and found to be believable. Others were dismissed at the time and only recognized many years later. Although few in number, the harmonic receptions provide an important glimpse into the desperate scene that played out on the reef at Gardner Island."[13]

Based on this testimony, TIGHAR speculated that Amelia and Fred had crash-landed just offshore from Nikumaroro. They had survived the crash and become castaways on the island, spending the next few days sending out radio messages and pleas for help. According to Ric Gillespie, the Director of TIGHAR, they could only use the radio when the tide was so low that it wouldn't flood the engine, limiting their access to the radio to just a few hours each night. He told the *Washington Post* that TIGHAR believed that Amelia and Fred died after becoming marooned on Nikumaroro, an island provided with coconuts, crabs, rodents, and birds, but lacking fresh water. This theory contradicts the official US Navy account, which claimed that the duo died after crashing into the Pacific Ocean just short of Howland Island, where they were scheduled to refuel.

In 2019, it appeared, for a moment, as though the mystery of Amelia and Fred's fate might have finally been solved. Researchers from Project Blue Angel announced that they were investigating the wreckage of an aircraft off the coast of Papua New Guinea. "We're still exploring to try to find out whose plane it is. We don't want to jump ahead and assume that it's Amelia's, but everything that we're seeing so far would tend to make us think it could be," said William Snavely, the director of the project. Snavely first learned of the site in 2005 from a local corrections officer from Buka Island. Then in 2011 the local government official asked him to investigate the wreck and determine where the aircraft had come from. He discovered several characteristics of Amelia's aircraft as well as a glass disc that may have been a light lens from the aircraft. "It has a rough shape and diameter that appears to be relatively consistent with lights that were on the plane back in the 1930s for Lockheed," said Snavely.[14] The wreckage is located along the route that Amelia and Fred would have flown. Snavely believes that Amelia and Fred flew for around 12 hours before turning around owing to low fuel.[15]

Project Blue Angel is currently in the process of raising funds so that they can embark on future dives to the wreckage and attempt further investigation. On their website, they stress that there is no conclusive proof that the wreckage is Amelia Earhart's aircraft.

Over the years, a number of somewhat fanciful theories have been put forward to explain Amelia Earhart's mysterious disappearance. One is that Amelia was working as a secret agent for the US government, having been enlisted to spy on Japan – even though her flight path never came close to Japan itself. This theory derives from Amelia's close relationship with Franklin D. Roosevelt and his wife, Eleanor. Another hypothesis is that Amelia Earhart was taken to Japan, where, as the infamous Tokyo Rose, she broadcasted anti-American propaganda to the world.

In their 1970 book *Amelia Earhart Lives,* Joe Klass and Joseph Gervais claimed that Amelia had survived the plane crash and then moved to New Jersey, where she changed her name to Irene Craigmile Bolam and worked as a banker. Irene completely denied the authors' claim, stating: "I am not Amelia Earhart!" and describing the book as "a poorly documented hoax".[16] *National Geographic* later hired a facial expert, who dismissed the theory that Amelia and Irene were the same person.

Perhaps the most plausible explanation is that Amelia Earhart and Fred Noonan ran out of fuel, crashed in the Pacific, and died on impact, the ocean's deep, dark waters concealing all evidence of the tragedy. "She ran out of gas and went down, no two ways about it," said Sally Putnam Chapman, granddaughter of Amelia's husband. "It was cloudy that day, she couldn't see the island, she wasn't sure where she was and went down." However, this theory, too, has been met with disbelief by those who have difficulty accepting such an unromantic end to the legend: "We have no evidence anywhere that she crashed into the ocean, even though that's been the common narrative for so many years," said former FBI Executive Assistant Director Shawn Henry. However, as Doris Rich, author of *Amelia Earhart: A Biography,* once said: "Maybe the American public doesn't want to lose the mystery. Maybe they'd rather keep it."[17]

The disappearance of Amelia Earhart and Fred Noonan – considered by some the Holy Grail of aviation mysteries – has captured the imaginations of professional and amateur sleuths across the globe. And while Amelia certainly wasn't the first female flyer, she captivated public attention like no other woman pilot before or since. Sadly, however, the mystery of her final flight has tended to overshadow her earlier accomplishments and those of the pioneering women who went before her.

With her disappearance, Amelia simultaneously became an icon and an elusive American legend. Nonetheless, her motto, "Women must try to do things as men have tried," still inspires young women to pursue their dreams today.

The Roswell Incident

Ever since the summer of 1947, the once-sleepy town of Roswell, New Mexico, has been a Mecca for UFO enthusiasts and conspiracy theorists. In July of that year, during a lightning storm, an alien spacecraft allegedly fell on a remote ranch. The incident sparked a plethora of rumours, speculation, and official denials, fuelling a passion for accounts of UFOs and extraterrestrial activity that rapidly spread all over the world.

"It's a modern myth, a kind of religion.
There is a common human need for salvation,
and it's always coming from above."

Robert A. Baker, UFO sceptic and former

psychology professor at the University of Kentucky

At some point during the first week of July 1947 (the date is disputed), Mac Brazel saddled his horse and rode deep into the J. B. Foster Ranch, near the village of Corona, around 120 km (75 miles) northwest of Roswell. Brazel worked as a foreman on the ranch and was accompanied by his seven-year-old neighbour, Dee Proctor, whom he paid 25 cents a day to help him out in the fields. While going about his duties, Brazel came across a large area of wreckage some 11 km (7 miles) from the small wooden ranch house. The wreckage consisted of metal, some of which was dull and some of which was shiny and thin, resembling tinfoil. There was also something that looked like transparent plastic string or wire, and thin sticks shaped like I-beams, made from a material that Brazel was unable to identify. He estimated that the wreckage extended over an area 1.2 km (three-quarters of a mile) long and 60 to 90 m (200 to 300 ft) wide. It appeared as though some kind of machine had exploded in mid-air and wreckage from it had rained down on the earth.

The area had been struck by violent thunderstorms the preceding night and Brazel had heard what he thought sounded like a loud explosion. He picked up several fragments of the wreckage and noticed that they were lightweight but unusually strong. He stuffed them into his pocket and continued with his work. Later that evening, Brazel dropped Proctor off at his home. The little boy showed his mother, Loretta, some of the fragments. Loretta recalled, "He had a piece of stuff about 5 or 6 inches long that looked like wood or plastic. It was a little bit bigger than a pencil and kind of a tannish colour. I remember Mac and my husband trying to whittle it with a knife and trying to burn it. It wouldn't burn and it wouldn't whittle."[1]

The discovery of the mysterious wreckage was the climax of several weeks of reports from across the country of strange circular discs seen skimming through the sky at high speed. Around the same time as the debris was discovered, four patients at the US Veterans Affairs hospital in Albuquerque, New Mexico, described how they watched a "flying disc" disappear into clouds and then reappear in the sky. The men, John Goyng, Charles Roat, Fred Lucero, and Lorenzo Garcia, described the object thus: "It seemed like a round ball, brighter than any airplane we've ever seen, and was going straight . . . not dipping. It had nothing projecting from it that we could see." Another local, Jess Stathrite, reported that he, too, had witnessed five saucer-shaped objects, one of which appeared to be circling the city.[2]

After hearing about these sightings, Brazel drove to Roswell to speak with Sheriff George Wilcox, believing that he might receive a reward for his discovery on the J. B. Foster Ranch. He described what he had found and "whispered kinda confidential-like" that he might have found one of these peculiar flying discs people had reported seeing. He had intended to keep fragments of the object until he had heard of recent bizarre sightings in the sky. Sheriff Wilcox contacted the Roswell Army Air Field to report Brazel's find. The base was the home of the 509th Bomb Group, the unit that had conducted the atomic bombings that devastated the Japanese cities of Hiroshima and Nagasaki just two years prior during World War II. Roswell was one of several top-secret military installations in the area.

Roswell Army Air Field commander Col. William Blanchard ordered his intelligence officer, Major Jesse Marcel, to accompany Brazel to view the debris found on the ranch. Following behind was counter-intelligence officer Sheridan Cavitt. They were ordered to collect as much of the wreckage as they could and bring it back to the base. According to First Lieutenant Walter Haut, Major Marcel described some of the material as "foil that you could take in your hand and crumple it up as tight as you could, and it would spring back to its original shape after you released it, without any creases". He also described "a 30-inch I-beam that they hit with a 19-pound sledgehammer, and it bounced off of it. And transparent wires that resembled today's fibre optics". In 1979, Major Marcel commented, "It was quite obvious to me . . . that it was not a weather balloon, nor was it an airplane, or a missile. What it was, we don't know."[3]

The following day, two more counter-intelligence officers and a number of soldiers arrived and cordoned off the area. While they gathered up the pieces of wreckage, Brazel was asked to accompany them back to Roswell. He was kept there for almost a week. "He would never talk about it after he came back," said Loretta Proctor. Following his ordeal, Brazel said that he would never report anything again "unless it was an atomic bomb".[4] According to some of Brazel's neighbours, following his return to the ranch, he was somehow able to purchase a new pickup truck and start a new business in Alamogordo, New Mexico, closer to where his family lived, in Tularosa.

The mysterious sightings and the wreckage led some Roswell citizens to speculate that a UFO had crashed near their little town. Others feared that the objects seen in the sky were something much more sinister – a Soviet secret weapon. A piece in the *Fort Lauderdale Daily News*, 7 July 1947, voiced this concern: "If the objects aren't Army or Navy devices then we are faced with a real mystery and one that our officials had better bear down on in a hurry. It wouldn't be the most comfortable feeling in the world to know that some foreign power has developed a way to penetrate this nation's skies at will . . ."

On 8 July 1947, a headline in the *Roswell Daily Record* boldly proclaimed, "RAAF Captures Flying Saucer on Ranch in Roswell Region."[4] Officials at Roswell Army Air Field had issued a news release reporting that they had recovered a crashed disc. It read:

"The many rumors regarding the flying disc became a reality yesterday when the intelligence office of the 509th Bomb Group of the 8th Air Force, Roswell Army Air Field, was fortunate enough to gain posses-sion of a disc through the cooperation of one of the local ranchers and the sheriff's office of Chaves County. The flying object landed on a ranch near Roswell sometime last week. Not having phone facilities, the rancher stored the disc until such time as he was able to contact the sheriff's office, who in turn notified Maj. Jesse A. Marcel of the 509th Bomb Group intelligence office. Action was immediately taken and the disc was picked up at the rancher's home. It was inspected at the Roswell Army Air Field and subsequently loaned by Major Marcel to higher headquarters."

Just the next day, however, Fort Worth Army Air Field refuted this announcement and claimed that the unidentified object was nothing more than debris from a crashed weather balloon. Irving Newton, the weather officer at Fort Worth Army Air Field, said that he had been ordered to the base commander's office to examine the crash debris. "I told them, 'That's a bunch of horse puckey – that's a radar target and a weather balloon. If it's not, I'll eat it, without salt and pepper.'"[5]

After being released from military custody, Brazel substantially changed his description of what he had found on the ranch. He now claimed that he had collected all the debris into two bundles that were less than 0.9 m (3 ft) long and 20 cm (8 in) thick, weighing around 2.3 kg (5 lb). He now described the debris as tinfoil, paper, sticky tape, sticks, and rubber. While Brazel had changed his version of events, in a subsequent interview with the *Record* and the *Associated Press*, Brazel potentially hinted at some kind of cover-up when he said that he had found two weather observation balloons in the past and was adamant that whatever this object was, it wasn't a weather observation balloon.[6]

Ever since, speculation about extraterrestrials and government cover-ups has become so widespread that the "Roswell Incident" has gained legendary status. According to some, the US military silencing their own reports of a "flying disc", combined with Brazel's revised description of what he found, marked the beginning of a government cover-up of evidence that something far more unusual crashed to earth. For sceptics, however, the Roswell Incident is a prime example of how a series of misunderstandings, poor research, and rumours can take on a life of their own and create an entirely false image of what was actually a commonplace event involving a weather observation balloon. "It's a modern myth, a kind of religion. There is a common human need for salvation, and it's always coming from above," said the noted UFO sceptic Robert A. Baker, professor of psychology emeritus at the University of Kentucky.

One of the most startling aspects of the Roswell Incident is the claim made by some Ufologists that the wreckage contained the dead bodies of extraterrestrials, and that these bodies were removed by the military for government study.

Stanton Friedman, a nuclear physicist who worked on government studies for a number of companies, began researching UFO sightings back in the 1950s. He and his partner, William Moore, came to the conclusion that the debris Brazel found was the remnants of a UFO crash. They deduced that an army pilot had witnessed the crash and called for soldiers to approach the scene and remove any dead bodies of extraterrestrials. In *Crash at Corona: The U.S. Military Retrieval and Cover-up of a UFO*, a 1992 book Friedman co-authored with science writer Don Berliner, Friedman suggests that a second UFO crashed at Magdalena, a village in New Mexico, around the same time, and that the US army recovered that craft as well, along with several bodies and at least one living extraterrestrial. In his book, Friedman quoted local farmer Barney Barnett, who was present at the alleged crash scene at Magdalena, as saying, "While we were looking at (the bodies), a military officer drove up in a truck with a driver and took control. He told everybody that the army was taking over and to get out of the way. Other military personnel came up and cordoned off the area. We were told to leave the area and not to talk to anyone about what we had seen . . . that it was our patriotic duty to remain silent."

Around six months after the incident, GI John Tilley arrived in Roswell. He later became an Air Force master sergeant and co-authored with Larry Tilley a book titled *Exposé: Roswell UFO Incident* in 2007. While at Roswell, Tilley heard an unnerving tale that was swirling around the base: "The scuttlebutt at the base was that something had escaped from the military, and that whatever had escaped had left the base and was peering through windows and scaring the heck out of people. That didn't mean anything to an 18-year-old kid from West Virginia. But four or five years ago, I met a UFO historian who told me that in UFO circles there has always been a whispered rumour that one of the four extraterrestrials that crashed at Corona was alive and that it escaped. And when the military located it near the base gate, they killed it. They were afraid of it. So you take that and put it together with what I heard, and what have you got?"[7]

In his book, Tilley writes that his brother-in-law, James Storm, was working as a member of the RAAF base fire department when he was involved with transporting the wreckage from the Roswell crash site back to the airbase. Storm claimed they were ordered to park off-road, out of sight, and wait. After several minutes, a "snub-nosed tractor and lowboy flat trailer showed up". He described how on the back of the trailer was a tarp covering an object. In Storm's own words to Tilley, it was "a saucer part so big that it [the trailer] was covered".[8]

In 1989, former US military intelligence officer Leonard H. Stringfield revealed that, four years earlier, he had spoken with Chris Coffey, a close friend of NASA astronomer Lt Col. Ellison Onizuka. Allegedly, Onizuka told Coffey that, while serving at McClellan Air Force Base in 1973, he was shown black-and-white footage of "alien bodies on a slab". Coffey claimed that Onizuka had intended to speak with Stringfield because he was a known Ufologist. However, before he could do so, Onizuka died in the Space Shuttle *Challenger* disaster of 28 January 1986.[9]

It later transpired that, shortly after he arrived at Roswell Army

Air Field to report his findings, Brazel himself had suggested that there were extraterrestrial bodies among the wreckage. The following excerpt is from a telephone conversation Brazel had with Frank Joyce, then an announcer on KGFL Radio, on 6 July 1947:

> Brazel: *"Who's gonna clean all that stuff up? That's what I wanna know. I need someone out there to clean it up."*
>
> Joyce: *"What stuff? What are you talking about?"*
>
> Brazel: *"Don't know. Don't know what it is. Maybe it's from one of them 'flying saucer' things."*
>
> Joyce: *"Oh really? Then you should call the air base. They are responsible for everything that flies in the air. They should be able to help you or tell you what it is."*
>
> Brazel: *"Oh, God. Oh, my God. What am I gonna do? It's horrible. Horrible. Just horrible."*
>
> Joyce: *"What's that? What's horrible? What are you talking about?"*
>
> Brazel: *"The stench. Just awful."*
>
> Joyce: *"Stench? From what? What are you talking about?"*
>
> Brazel: *"They're dead."*
>
> Joyce: *"What? Who's dead?"*
>
> Brazel: *"Little people. Unfortunate little creatures . . ."*[10]

KGFL had planned to run with the story and bring Brazel in for an interview, but before they had the chance, soldiers took Brazel to Roswell Army Air Field. KGFL was threatened that if they released any portion of the recording, they would lose their broadcasting licence.

The widespread belief of a cover-up led US Republican Congressman Steven Schiff to request information from the Pentagon about the Roswell Incident. The Pentagon's lacklustre response encouraged Schiff to accuse the authorities of stonewalling. In 1993, Schiff asked the federal government's General Accounting Office for a full and honest investigation into the Roswell Incident. In a letter to Secretary of Defense Les Aspin, he wrote:

"Last fall, I became aware of a strange series of events beginning in New Mexico over 45 years ago and involving personnel of what was then the Army Air Force. I have since reviewed the facts in some detail, and I am writing to request your assistance in arriving at a definitive explanation of what transpired and why."

The US Air Force allegedly launched an official inquiry before releasing a report. The report claimed that the debris found near Corona was related to Project Mogul, a top-secret programme using balloons to spy on Soviet nuclear tests. They claimed that the wreckage was part of a 183-m (600-ft) balloon train that was used to detect Russian nuclear blasts and reflect signals back to tracking stations. The report introduced Charles Moore, a scientist who worked on Project Mogul, as its key witness. Moore claimed that the balloons were equipped with corner reflectors that were put together with beams made from balsa wood and coated with synthetic resin glue similar to that made by Elmer, to strengthen them. They claimed that this was the peculiar material found at the crash site that neither Major Marcel or Brazel could identify.

The report also noted that "many of the persons making the biggest claims of alien bodies make their living from the 'Roswell Incident'". The US Air Force later released another statement that suggested that the so-called extraterrestrial corpses allegedly seen at the crash site were likely "a combination of innocently transformed memories of military accidents involving injured or killed personnel, innocently transformed memories of the recovery of andromorphic dummies in military programs like Operation High Dive conducted in the 1950s, and hoaxes perpetrated by various witnesses and UFO proponents".[11]

Despite these reports, rumours about extraterrestrials and UFOs connected to Roswell still had plenty of traction both in the US and around the world. Many people refused to accept the official version and dismissed it as a new and improved whitewash. "I think the Air Force is truly getting desperate," said Stanton Friedman. "None of that work (with test dummies) was done before the 1950s."[12]

In 1995, the Fox Network aired a documentary titled *Alien Autopsy: Fact or Fiction?* The programme featured a grainy 17-minute film that, it was claimed, depicted surgeons performing an autopsy on one of the extraterrestrials recovered from the wreckage. A British businessman, Ray Santilli, said that he had purchased the film from a former US Army photographer while on a trip to Cleveland in 1992. Many people – including scientists and movie special-effects artists – were unconvinced by the footage and labelled it a hoax. Around the same time, however, a CNN/Time poll revealed that the majority of people interviewed still believed that extraterrestrials had visited Earth but that the government was covering it up. In 2006, Santilli confessed that the footage was a reconstruction. He still claimed that he had seen real footage of the autopsy but that most frames had been destroyed and then lost, so he decided that he would recreate the footage.

However, controversy concerning the Roswell Incident did not end there. In 1999, former Deputy Sheriff Charles H. Forgus made a shocking revelation about the wreckage. According to Forgus, he had been driving from Texas to Roswell with Sheriff Jess Slaughter to pick up a prisoner on the night of the crash near Corona when they heard reports of a crashed aircraft over their radio. The two sheriffs decided to investigate. Forgus claimed that he saw bodies of at least four extraterrestrials at the crash site. He described them as being approximately 1.5 m (5 ft) tall with large eyes and feet not dissimilar to those of humans. He also said that they had brownish skin and that he saw no blood.[13]

Forgus claimed that there were around three to four hundred soldiers in the area but he could not identify them as US Air Force personnel. "When we got there, the land was covered with soldiers," he recollected. "They were hauling a big creature." Shortly afterward, the soldiers told Forgus and Slaughter to leave the area. Forgus said that, following this bizarre encounter, he was approached by government officials and told to keep quiet. Forgus' testimony was not revealed until 2017 when it was released at the same time as the book *UFOS Today: 70 Years of Lies, Disinformation, and Government Cover-up* by Dr Irena Scott. "The Great Father didn't just make this planet . . . He made all of them. He put beings on these planets just like he put us on this one. They're smarter than we are," remarked Forgus. "They can get from there to here, but we can't get from here to there."

That same year – 2017 – a CIA agent suffering from kidney failure made a deathbed confession to Richard Dolan, author of *UFOs and the National Security State: Chronology of a Cover-up, 1941–1973.* Dolan's interview with the agent was recorded; but the agent himself, who claimed that he had previously served in the US Army and also worked on a US Air Force official investigation into UFO activity, Project Blue Book, was never publicly named. The agent claimed to have seen the crashed UFO and the bodies of extraterrestrials. He also said that the UFO was kept in the top-secret Area 51 facility of the USAF base at the Nevada Test and Training Range for quite a while.

The same book by Dolan features an account by Glenn Dennis, a mortician in Roswell at the time. According to Dennis, in early July 1947, he received several phone calls from the Roswell AAF mortuary officer inquiring about embalming chemicals and their effects on internal organs. Dennis was also asked about hermetically sealed caskets and how small they came. "He also wanted to know about procedures for picking up bodies that had been left in the elements for several days, possibly mutilated by predators. I asked if I could help. He declined."[14]

The Ballard Funeral Home, where Dennis worked, also functioned as an ambulance service. Later that same evening, Dennis drove to the base infirmary a GI who had been in an accident. After dropping the soldier inside, Dennis walked around back to see a nurse that he was friendly with. She warned him that he shouldn't be there and even told him that he was going to get himself killed. Moments later, "a big, red-headed colonel" said, "What's that son of a bitch doing here?" The colonel then escorted Dennis off the base and told him to keep his mouth shut. The next day, Dennis spoke with the nurse again and she told him that she had seen three little bodies – two of which were badly mangled while the other was in good condition. "She also said on one gurney were two crash bags with two mutilated bodies inside. She said they had a horrible smell," recollected Dennis. The nurse was never identified, but shortly afterwards, she was transferred to England. She later died in a plane crash.[15]

Despite the fact that the debris was found closest to the village of Corona, it is the city of Roswell that has become forever linked to these extraordinary events. When visitors enter Roswell, stickers or figures of little green extraterrestrials peer from windows and store fronts. Two UFO museums – the International UFO Museum and Research Center and The Roswell UFO Spacewalk – opened in the town and were instant hits. "Since I got involved here, a lot of my personal pursuits have taken a back seat. This thing has taken off so fast," said former Roswell mortician Glenn Dennis, who became vice president of the International UFO Museum and Research Center before his death, aged 90, in 2015.[16] Each year the city holds a weeklong UFO Festival that contributes millions of dollars to the local economy.

The Roswell Incident mesmerized the world and remains a cornerstone of UFO lore. Whatever may have transpired in 1947 offers genuine hope to those seeking to prove that extraterrestrials not only exist, but have visited this planet.

The Flatwoods Monster

An unidentified flying object flashing across the West Virginia sky and seemingly falling to earth prompted a local family and their friends to investigate. Before long, they would come face to face with the bizarre, frightening creature that has since achieved legendary status as the "Flatwoods Monster".

"Things that people can't explain, they just don't want to accept or have any belief in."

Flatwoods historian and retired schoolteacher Judith Davis

The bizarre story of the Flatwoods Monster began on the evening of 12 September 1952, in the small village of Flatwoods, Braxton County, West Virginia. It was around 7 pm when some boys playing football on the local school playground saw what they described as a bright, oval-shaped object land on a nearby hilltop, belonging to a farm owned by G. Bailey Fisher.

The boys rushed to the home of Kathleen May, mother of two of the boys. Some of the boys were adamant that they had seen a flying saucer, while others said it was probably just a meteor. Several of them stated that the object looked like a silver dollar spouting an exhaust trail that resembled red balls of fire. They also said it had come from the southwest.[1] Kathleen May told the excited group that they were just imagining things. Then she looked towards the hill and spotted a strange red glow in the sky. Grabbing a torch, because dusk was falling, she and the boys set off to investigate. The group consisted of Kathleen; her two sons, Eddie, 13, and Freddie, 14; Neil Nunley, 14; Tommy Hyer, 10; Ronnie Shaver, 10; and National Guard member Gene Lemon, 17.

As Lemon led the party up the hill, he noticed that the path in front of them was shrouded by a strange, low-rolling fog. The fog curled around the trees and soon enough engulfed the entire area ahead of them. "It was very hazy in the area along the path. It was also very misty along the tree area," recalled Freddie. It wasn't the typical evening fog that settled through the mountains, but instead appeared to be emanating from a specific source. Undeterred, the group carried on through the fog and noticed that there was a strong odour in the air, similar to burning sulphur, which irritated their eyes and nostrils. Nevertheless, the party continued up the hill. Suddenly they were stopped in their tracks by an eerie sight: a pair of bright-red eyes in a tree.

At first, they thought that the eyes were simply those of an opossum or raccoon perched on a tree branch. However, Lemon and May both shone their flashlights toward the gleaming eyes – to reveal what Lemon described as "a 10-foot [3-m] monster with a blood-red face and green body that seemed to glow."[2] As their torch beams illuminated the monster, its glowing eyes projected a powerful beam of light towards the group. Terrified, Lemon let out a deafening scream and fell backwards.

Kathleen recounted that the monster was around 4 ft (1.2m) wide and started moving towards them with a floating, bouncing motion. "It just moved. It didn't walk. It moved evenly. It didn't jump. It was kind of floating. It was about a foot to a foot and a half off the ground, but it didn't have any kind of feet or anything that we could see." As it came closer, Kathleen registered a pungent mist and "an overpowering, gaseous smell that burned my nostrils and made me feel sick." The group turned and ran for home, but not before the monster spewed what appeared to be an oily fluid onto the ground, some of which spattered their clothing. "Nobody said anything – everybody ran," recollected Lemon. "We just got a good look at it and left."

Back at Kathleen's house, they telephoned the Braxton County Sheriff's Department in the nearby town of Sutton, but were informed that Sheriff Robert Carr and his deputy were near Frametown, investigating a reported plane crash. Meanwhile, several of the group started to feel ill. Lemon was particularly badly affected during the night, experiencing convulsions and vomiting attacks. The throats of the May brothers were so swollen that they were unable to drink water. When Kathleen took them to the doctor the next morning, his examination revealed that they had symptoms similar to mustard-gas poisoning.

The group soon reported what they had seen to the police and the local press. Kathleen May and Gene Lemon described the figure they had seen as having the shape of a man, but with a blood-red, heart-shaped head with a distinct point at the top. They added that the monster had a bright-green body that appeared to give off a strange light and a pungent smell, similar to rotten eggs, that burned their eyes and nostrils. It looked "worse than Frankenstein" said Kathleen. "It couldn't have been human."[3] As the monster floated towards them, they said it emitted a loud shrieking and hissing sound, like the sound of frying bacon. Others of the group claimed that the monster was dark in colour, while one of the boys said, "The monster was obviously black really, but as it was hot. It was getting red hot like a poker."

The police laughed off the group's statements as mass hysteria. They also dismissed the so-called flying saucer as simply a meteor, claiming that there had recently been a meteor shower across a three-state area. The monster was probably an animal in a tree, glowing in reflected light. "The rest was pure imagination," said Sheriff Robert Carr.[4]

The locals were torn between believers and sceptics. A. Lee

Stewart, Jr, co-publisher of the *Braxton Democrat*, organized an armed posse, who set off to investigate the following morning. "The odour was still there," he recalled. "It was sort of warm and sickening." In addition to the strange, unpleasant smell, he discovered skid marks and "two places about six to eight feet in diameter where the brush was trampled down." Alongside the flattened grass and skid marks were traces of "an odd gummy deposit".[5] While Stewart couldn't explain the odour, he reported back that he couldn't quite believe the group's claims of a monster.[6] He did say, however, that the group that claimed to have seen the monster were "scared – bad scared".

The following day, several newspapers ran pieces about the alleged monster. Police Capt. J. B. Jack told reporters that investigators had failed to find anything that could shed further light on the story and had found no evidence of a monster or a UFO. Mayor J. Holt Byrne speculated that the so-called monster was nothing more than "vapour" that could have come from a meteor. He said that a meteor could account for the strange object the boys saw in the sky, as well as the bad odour.[7] However, no meteor fragments were found at the scene.

The *Baltimore Sun* individually interviewed the key witnesses – Kathleen, Eddie, and Freddie May; Neil Nunley; Tommy Hyer; Ronnie Shaver; and Gene Lemon. They each drew pictures of what they had seen and described the monster as being around 10 to 12 feet (3 to 3.7m) tall, stating that they could tell how tall it was because the top of its head was level with a certain branch on the tree. Several of them also described a large object that they had spotted alongside the monster: a truncated cone or globe with a smaller cone or globe on top of it with a circular transparent window in front, from which a small blue spotlight shone out. Neil Nunley described the object as more like "a big ball of fire", as opposed to a cone or globe. As the group turned to run back home, they described how the monster started to glide towards this large, glowing object. The *Baltimore Sun*'s report concluded by confirming that the drawing of the glowing object and the Flatwoods Monster was sent to the Air Force District of Washington (AFDW), which had responded that it would not be investigating the strange occurrence.[8]

A week after the sighting, Kathleen May and Gene Lemon appeared on *We the People*, a national television show, to talk about their experience. A sketch artist drew a representation of the monster based on their descriptions. However, this drawing did not match what May and Lemon said they had seen. The artist sensationally portrayed the monster as having large claws and a hooded garment and dress.[9]

According to Frank Feschino Jr, author of *The Braxton County Monster: The Cover-Up of the Flatwoods Monster Revealed* and *Shoot Them Down! The Flying Saucer Air Wars of 1952*, his research and interviews with the Flatwoods witnesses led him to conclude that the monster was not a flesh-and-blood being but a metal-like structure, similar to a rocket or possibly even a creature in a suit. "It had great big eyes, portholes, or whatever you want to call them . . . And basically, it was funny-looking orange in the portholes," May told Feschino. May's son, Freddie, also told Feschino that "over the head was a big ace of spades covering", adding that it "was something that looked like a helmet". Over the years, the description of the monster in the media has become wildly distorted. "I don't think there are two stories about the Flatwoods Monster that are the same," observed Feschino.

At the time, the authorities did take the Flatwoods Monster seriously enough to mount an investigation. Federal investigators and scientists visited the scene and took pictures and soil samples. However, the results were never released.

A few weeks after the sighting, Kathleen May received a letter from the Pentagon, along with a picture of what they claimed she and the rest of the group must have seen in the woods that evening. The object they had encountered was a "moon landing vehicle", which was supposedly being test-flown over desolate regions of the country. The letter explained that whenever the vehicle had to land, pilots would typically choose areas that were uninhabited, but on 12 September, they had mistakenly landed in Flatwoods. The letter also stated that the group that had spotted the object in the woods were the very first civilians to ever see the vehicle.[10]

Intriguingly, the Flatwoods group were not the only people to witness a strange phenomenon in the area. At around 8 pm the following evening, 13 September, George and Edith Snitowsky from New York were driving between the towns of Gassaway and Frametown, West Virginia, with their 18-month-old son when their car stalled. As George tried to restart the engine, a sickening smell overpowered them. George described this odour as, "like a mixture of ether and burned sulphur". Suddenly, a violet beam of light, emanating from a wooded area bordering the desolate road, illuminated their car. George got out to investigate, but as he drew closer to the light, he experienced the "sensation of thousands of needle-like vibrations" on his skin.[11] The sensation – like an electric shock – was so strong that George buckled at the knees. Unwilling to venture any closer, George staggered back to the car.

As George approached the vehicle, he saw his wife, Edith, frozen in fear in the passenger's seat. She was staring out of the window over George's shoulder. George turned and saw a terrifying sight: "A figure . . . standing immobile, on the fringe of the road, about

30 feet [9 m] to my right." He described the figure as around 8 or 9 feet (2.4 or 2.7m) tall. It had the general shape of a man, with a head, shoulders, and a bloated body. He also said that the figure had "long, spindly arms" and was gliding rapidly towards him. George managed to jump back into the car and the family huddled together as the figure came closer. They looked on in horror as one of its arms stretched across their windscreen, as if inspecting their car. George saw that the end of its arm was forked. The creature then glided back towards the woods. Moments later, George and Edith saw a glowing globe, swaying back and forth as it lifted above the trees and vanished into the dark sky. Their car now started without a problem.

The following morning, after a night of broken sleep at a motel in the town of Sutton, the couple noticed a burnt spot on the bonnet of their car that had not been there before. This bizarre experience terrified George and Edith so much that they didn't report what they had witnessed until 1955, when George recounted his experience in *Male Magazine*, a publication specializing in sensational stories.

Since then, the Flatwoods Monster has become one of the most curious unexplained events in UFO history, intriguing scientists, paranormal investigators, and conspiracy theorists all over the world. Some maintain that the monster was simply a product of mass hysteria. Others, however, are convinced that the sighting was of an extraterrestrial. "Things that people can't explain, they just don't want to accept or have any belief in," said Judith Davis, a Flatwoods historian and retired schoolteacher who, accompanying herself on an autoharp, used to entertain her students with a song about the monster titled "The Phantom of Flatwoods".

Over the years, one of the most common theories is that the

object spotted in the sky that night was a meteor shower. Dr Joe Nickell of the Committee for the Scientific Investigation of Claims of the Paranormal suggested that the group had witnessed a meteor shower and then spotted an owl in the tree with the underbrush below it, giving the impression of a much larger figure. However, Harvard Meteor Project, which tracked 2,500 meteors between 1952 and 1954, recorded no meteor activity on that specific date. Furthermore, there was no shock wave, no crater, and no meteorite fragments found anywhere in Flatwoods or the surrounding area. In addition, the owl theory did not explain the presence of the foul-smelling odour and the oil-like substance found at the scene and on the group's clothing. Stanton Friedman, a nuclear physicist who worked on government studies for a number of companies, described the meteor and owl theory as "trying to fit a square peg into a round hole". The astronomer Hal Povenmire, author of *Fireballs, Meteors, and Tektites,* told *Florida Today*: "It definitely wasn't a meteor."

Ufologists are convinced that, that night, the group experienced a genuine "close encounter of the third kind" – an encounter with a UFO and an extraterrestrial lifeform – with added elements of US government cover-up. The reported sighting of the Flatwoods Monster coincided with a wave of UFO reports throughout Braxton County and a number of other Eastern states, including Pennsylvania, Ohio, Tennessee, Maryland, and Washington, DC. In fact, there were 21 hours of UFO sightings on 12 September 1952. Many people reported objects blazing through the sky. Some thought that they were witnessing an aeroplane crashing in a fireball. Former Flatwoods Mayor Margaret Clise recalled that, as she was walking to her grandparents' home, she "saw this thing that looked like a burning star".[12] The sight disturbed her so much that she broke a bowl she was carrying as she rushed to get inside the house. Later, she said she noticed the tops of several trees in the area appeared to be scorched. "Some people insisted it was a meteorite, but they never found a meteorite," she said. "Some people think it was just a figment of everyone's imagination, which is impossible, because too many people saw it. We know something happened. We just don't know what it was."[13]

On the same day as the Flatwoods Monster sighting, there were reports of the loss of an F-94 Sabrejet pilot and radar operator. John A. Jones and John S. DelCurto were reported missing after they took off from Tyndall Air Force Base in Panama City to conduct a "local, routine training flight". According to news articles at the time, the men had reported bad weather and were ordered to land at Moody AFB in Georgia before losing contact and presumably crashing after running out of fuel. On the night of the Flatwoods Monster sighting, the West Virginia National Guard was mobilized in Braxton County under the direction of the United States Air Force. National Guard troops were also mobilized in the Frametown area to search for evidence of a crashed aeroplane. This was why, when Kathleen May called the Braxton County Sheriff's office, she was informed he was in Frametown, searching for a downed aircraft.

When Feschino attempted to locate the official records of the disappearance through military archives, he was met with a bureaucratic runaround and informed that no records of the incident existed. However, he did discover that other accident reports from that time were often incomplete or missing at the National Archives, and words such as "disappeared" and "disintegrated" quite often appeared in news accounts of these events. According to Feschino, the US Air Force changed the time of the disappearance, presumably so it did not coincide with the sighting of the Flatwoods Monster. In Feschino's book *Shoot Them Down: The Flying Saucer Air Wars of 1952*, he revealed a disturbing number of fatal air engagements and a number of disappearances of veteran combat pilots along with their aircraft.

After investigating the case for over a decade, Feschino came to the conclusion that "as many as 20" American planes had been attacked and shot down by UFOs and that the multiple sightings of UFOs that night had been a "rescue mission" by UFOs to salvage a damaged UFO. Feschino came to this remarkable conclusion after tracking down and interviewing numerous eyewitnesses and military and government sources. He believed that the objects people saw in the sky that night were 16 UFOs in groups of four. He contends that the Truman administration gave the Air Force orders to seek and destroy the UFOs to alleviate mounting public tensions over the spate of mysterious sightings in the sky. "Of course you could cover this up. They do it all the time. Look at all the planes that got shot down during the Cold War on missions that supposedly did not exist. They made up cover stories and told the families back home all sorts of lies."

Feschino recreated a possible scenario for the night of 12 September 1952 by carefully plotting each UFO sighting from that night. He then compared the reported sightings with the official explanation of the event and spoke with military sources who knew about the incident. "I had to read between the lines of the government cover-up," he said. At the time, the US was locked in a Cold War with the Soviet Union and people were starting to realize that Russians could fly over the country and could poten-tially drop an atomic bomb.[14] Feschino believed that at least one of the UFOs was damaged by the US Air Force and crash-landed in Flatwoods. According to Feschino, the first sighting of the

The Lost Colony of Roanoke

This contemporary map shows the location of Roanoke Island; added details include native inhabitants and a party of colonists arriving in a boat.

Governor John White returns from England to discover the colony of Roanoke in ruins.

A sign proudly commemorates Virginia Dare's birth for posterity.

A 19th-century engraving records a momentous event for the colonists: the baptism of Virginia Dare.

The Mystery of the *Mary Celeste*

An 1861 illustration of the *Mary Celeste* when the ship was called *Amazon*.

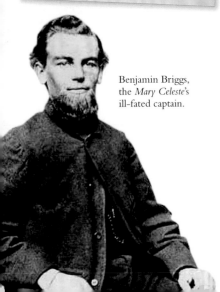

A sea monster attack was one of the more fanciful explanations for the absent crew.

Benjamin Briggs, the *Mary Celeste*'s ill-fated captain.

"THE APPEARANCES OF THE TABLE SHOWED THAT FOUR PERSONS HAD RISEN FROM A HALF-EATEN MEAL TO LEAVE THE CABIN FOR EVER."

The scene in the captain's cabin that allegedly confronted the crew of the *Dei Gratia* when they boarded the *Mary Celeste*.

The Flannan Lighthouse Mystery

The modern, automated Flannan Lighthouse on Eilean Mòr.

This contemporary (c.1900) photograph captures the homey, but cramped, living conditions endured by the three Flannan Lighthouse keepers.

The mystery of the lighthouse keepers' fate was dramatized in this 2018 movie starring Gerard Butler, Peter Mullan, and Connor Swindells.

The Disappearance of Amelia Earhart

On her first attempt at an around-the-world flight, Amelia Earhart's Lockheed 10-E Electra takes off from Oakland, California, for Honolulu.

Amelia Earhart's disappearance was front-page news.

Amelia with her navigator, Fred Noonan, Honolulu Airport, Hawaii, March 1937.

Technical problems with the aircraft frustrated her first around-the-world attempt, but Amelia Earhart's determination remained undimmed.

Amelia Earhart's aviation exploits secured her place in the record books, while her free-spirited courage inspired women all over the world.

The Roswell Incident

Since July 1947, Roswell has generated accusations of government cover-up, such as this protest in Washington DC, March 29, 1995.

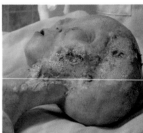

A close-up of an alien head in the International UFO Museum and Research Center, Roswell.

Air Force intelligence officer Jesse Marcel displays UFO debris from the Roswell site.

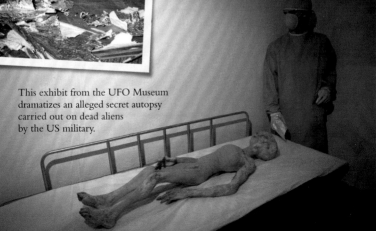

This exhibit from the UFO Museum dramatizes an alleged secret autopsy carried out on dead aliens by the US military.

The woods of West
Virginia, the scene of
alleged UFO activity
in September 1952.

An artist's impression
of the Flatwoods
Monster, based on
witnesses' accounts.

The Dyatlov Pass Incident

Igor Dyatlov

The leader of the tragic group that encountered disaster and death in the Siberian wilderness.

In this 2013 horror film, a band of American students attempts to investigate the Dyatlov Pass mystery.

This image taken by one of the hikers shows the group setting up camp around 5pm on February 2, 1959.

The group's flattened tent, as found by the rescue team on February 26, 1959.

The body of the expedition's leader, Igor Dyatlov.

An artist's impression of the aliens who abducted the Hills, based on their accounts while under hypnosis.

An artist captures Barney and Betty Hill's encounter with a UFO on a deserted road in New Hampshire in September 1961.

Betty and Barney Hill pose with a newspaper account headlined "New Hampshire UFO Chiller."

Dr Benjamin Simon conducts one of the Hills' hypnosis sessions.

Flatwoods Monster was the creature encased in a protective metallic suit and the second sighting, by the Snitowskys, was of the creature partially out of its suit.[15]

In 1975, Ufologist Major Donald Keyhoe documented in his book *Aliens from Space* that many reported UFO sightings from around the same time were covered up by the government. Much like Feschino, Keyhoe believed that the military had scrambled jets to intercept the UFOs, which were violating United States airspace. He said that Pentagon sources had told him that a spate of unexplained fatal air accidents had occurred as a reprisal for an attempt to shoot down a UFO by US Air Force jets.[16]

Despite the evidence of UFO activity all over the eastern United States on the night of the Flatwoods Monster, government officials continued to explain away the sightings as deriving from a single meteor. How a single meteor could have been seen in so many different places, at different times and going in different directions remains a mystery.

A final theory is that the Flatwoods Monster was a manifestation of the bizarre natural phenomenon ball lightning. This supposition was put forward by Paul Sagan in his 2004 book *Ball Lightning: Paradox of Physics*, in which he interviewed the Flatwoods Monster witnesses. Ball lightning varies in appearance from translucent to multicoloured, and has been observed at altitude (the Flatwoods Monster was encountered on a hilltop), near power lines, during thunderstorms, and even, apparently, on sunny days. It has been reported as hovering or moving in erratic ways, also exploding, making a hissing noise and leaving a sulphurous smell (both reported by the original Flatwoods group).

Whatever the witnesses encountered that night in Flatwoods truly remains a mystery, but it has become an essential part of local folklore. In fact, the Flatwoods Monster has become something of a mascot for Flatwoods' population of around 270 citizens. Signs at both ends of town read, "Welcome to Flatwoods. Home of the Green Monster." To nurture the Flatwoods legend and attract tourists, the Flatwoods Museum opened in Sutton in October 2017. There, visitors can learn all about the Flatwoods Monster, as described by the original witnesses, and purchase memorabilia, including mugs, figurines, t-shirts, baby clothes, even a spectacular, throne-like Flatwoods chair representing the fiery-eyed monster. Colby White, a Morgantown-based musician, was so inspired by the Flatwoods Monster that he has a tattoo of it on his forearm. He is one of many locals who believe the hype. "Here comes a bunch of kids, a woman shining a flashlight in this dude's eyes or this creature's eyes. Next thing he knows he's getting blinded and freaks out and starts vibrating and basically throws up some weird oil on them. So, I think they startled him. That's my theory, I think they startled the Flatwoods Monster," he declared.[17]

The captivating story of the Flatwoods Monster dominated the front pages of local newspapers for weeks on end, putting Braxton County firmly on the map. While some view the Flatwoods Monster as little more than a tall tale, others contend that there is some truth to the legend. "That night, they saw something that scared the heck out of them. It's hard to tell what can become a monster. We want people to think whatever they want to think," said Andrew Smith, director of the Braxton County Convention and Visitors Bureau.[18]

The Dyatlov Pass Incident

In the winter of 1959 eight men and two women vanished in Russia's Ural mountains. When a search and rescue team discovered their bodies, some were half-naked and barefoot, others had suspicious-looking injuries. The cause of those tragic, unaccountable deaths remains a source of often dark controversy. The incident has become one of Russia's best-known unsolved mysteries; in honour of the dead hikers, the area has been renamed Dyatlov Pass.

*"If I had a chance to ask God just
one question, it would be,
'What really happened to my
friends that night?'"*

Yuri Yudin, the sole survivor

On the morning of 25 January 1959, ten students and recent graduates from the Ural Polytechnic University – all experienced hikers and skiers – set off for the northern, 1,079-m (3,540-ft) summit of Russia's Ural Mountains. The route the group planned was long and the Siberian weather was harsh: They planned to ski 322 km (200 miles) over 16 days, scaling several peaks along the way. Each member relished the challenge, having previously completed tough expeditions and lengthy ski tours in the region. The party consisted of: Igor Alekseievich Dyatlov, the leader, 23; Zinaida Alekseevna Kolmogorova, 22; Lyudmila Alexandrovna Dubinina, 20; Aleksander Sergeievich Kolevatov, 23; Yuri Alexeievich Krivonischenko, 23; Yuri Doroshenko, 21; Nicolai Vladimirovich Thibeaux-Brignolles, 23; Seymon Alexandrovich Zolotaryov, 38; Rustem Vladimirovich Slobodin, 23; and Yuri Yudin, 22.

The group boarded a train at Ivdel, a town in the province of Sverdlovsk (now Yekaterinburg), then heading to Vizhay, the last inhabited settlement on their route, by truck. Unable to hitch a ride until the following morning, they stayed in Vizhay overnight. Here, Yuri Yudin contracted dysentery and was forced to turn back, leaving the other nine skiers to continue the expedition. Unbeknown to Yuri, this unfortunate illness would save his life.

Before leaving, Dyatlov had agreed to send a telegram to the Sverdlovsk Sports Committee as soon as the group returned to the village of Vizhay. He estimated that this would be around 12 February. Due to the harsh conditions, he had warned that the expedition's return might take somewhat longer, so when that date came and went and Dyatlov still had not made contact, no one was particularly surprised. The skiers were no amateurs. A week went by and still the group's families were reasonably unconcerned. However, by the end of the second week, it was evident that something was seriously wrong.

The Executive Committee of the Regional Council assembled a volunteer search and rescue team, who were assisted by sapper soldiers as well as aviation support. They struggled through heavy snow and bad weather until, on 26 February, they came upon the group's abandoned tent in an area near Gora Otorten, ominously known by the local Mansi people as Kholat Syakhl or "Mountain of Death". The tent was flapping in the wind and had been sliced open with a knife from the inside. Days of snow had accumulated on top of it. The group members were nowhere to be seen. The tent appeared to have been abandoned in a great hurry. Inside, clothing was neatly folded and boots tidily grouped. A bag containing bread and cereal was in one corner and an open flask of cocoa sat near the stove, as if ready to be reheated and drunk.[1] The search and rescue team also found a camera and diaries. The searchers sighed with relief that there were no bodies. Then they realized the awful truth. It would have been next to impossible for anyone to survive for long outside the tent.

The search revealed nine sets of footprints outside the tent.

Bizarrely, these footprints indicated that those that made them were either barefoot or wearing just one shoe. The prints led to a dense forest, but disappeared after around 500 m (550 yds).

The first two bodies were discovered on the forest edge. Krivonischenko and Doroshenko were both barefoot and dressed only in their underwear. Nearby, the searchers found evidence of a fire and damage to the branches of a pine tree, as if somebody had attempted to climb it, perhaps to determine their way back to the tent. The bodies of Dyatlov, Kolmogorova and Slobodin were then spotted, scattered respectively 300 m (330 yds), 480 m (525 yds), and 630 m (690 yds) between the tree and the tent. It appeared as though they had been attempting to return to the tent. Despite the sub-zero temperatures, the bodies were only partially clothed and most were missing shoes. Some were face down in the snow, others were curled in a foetal position. The final four bodies – Thibeaux-Brignolles, Kolevatov, Zolotaryov, and Dubinina – were discovered two months later, when the snow began to thaw. They were found at the bottom of a forest ravine around 75 m (80 yds) away from where the first two bodies were discovered. They were wearing more clothing than the others. It appeared that the first five had either given their clothes to these four or, more likely, they had died first and the other four had set off clothed in hopes of surviving the bitter cold. Zolotaryov was wearing Dubinina's fur coat and hat while Dubinina herself, whose body was lying in what was now a stream, had wrapped her feet in pieces of Krivonischenko's woollen pants.

The bodies were transported back to civilization, where an autopsy confirmed that six of the nine skiers had died from hypothermia, while three had met more brutal deaths. While none of the corpses showed evidence of a struggle, external injuries or bruising, Thibeaux-Brignolles and Slobodin both had fractured skulls; Dubinina and Zolotaryov had broken ribs; Dubinina was also missing her tongue and eyes. The internal injuries that they had sustained were not unlike those sustained in a high-impact car accident, which can occur without external indications. Thibeaux-Brignolles, Dubinina, and Zolotaryov had died from their injuries, while Slobodin had died from hypothermia; his skull fracture was a contributing factor, but not sufficiently severe to cause death.

The expedition had employed cameras and diaries to document their journey. These revealed that the group had skied through desolate mountains and across frozen lakes until it reached the edge of the low-altitude highlands on 31 January and prepared to climb. They traversed the mountain pass but, during the following day, they were caught in a snowstorm and became lost on the slopes of Kholat Syakhl, 10 km (6 miles) south of Otorten. When they real-ized that they had strayed from their route, they decided to pitch their tent on the mountainside for the night. Why Dyatlov chose this location is a mystery. It was at a height of 1,000 m (3,280 ft); if they had continued a little further, they would have been able to make camp in a safer location, beside a forest.[2] Photographs depicted the group pitching their tent at around 5 pm. The final diary entry indicated that the members were in good spirits. Yet something happened later that night that forced them to run, seemingly panic-stricken, from the warmth of their tent into the freezing cold.

Investigators were stumped. The skiers were familiar with the treacherous slopes of the Ural mountains, so what could have caused them to flee their tent to almost certain death? It was thought that the members had regrouped after leaving the tent and, as Dyatlov was the leader, he may have volunteered to venture back to the tent to collect clothing and other items they needed to survive. Slobodin and Kolmogorova may have accompanied him, all three falling victim to the elements before reaching camp. The rest may have sought shelter, before perishing in the harsh conditions. However, the severe injuries sustained by some of the group remained a mystery. A Soviet military inquest concluded that six had died of hypothermia, while three had died of major internal injuries. The lead investigator ruled that the cause of death was an "unknown compelling force". The case was classified as secret, routine in the Soviet Union at the time. The mountain was closed to the public for the next three years. A private investigation was briefly conducted, but called off in May.

The collapse of the Soviet Union in the latter half of the 1980s lifted the curtain of official silence. For decades, few people beyond the skiers' families were even aware of the tragic event. In 1990, Lev Ivanov, an investigator who had originally worked on the case, now known as the Dyatlov Pass Incident after the group's leader, wrote an article titled "Secret of the Fireballs" for the newspaper *Leninskit Put*. Ivanov suggested that the group had been killed by some kind of energy from fireballs that had been spotted in the sky around the time of the ill-fated expedition. On 18 February 1959, the *Nizhny Tagil* newspaper reported that a fireball had been spotted in the skies of Nizhny Tagil, heading towards the northern peak of the Ural mountains. "At 7:00 a flash appeared inside it, and the very bright core of the ball became visible. It began to glow more intensively, and was enshrouded in a luminous cloud, elongated toward the south," read part of the article.[3] Ivanov confessed that, at the time of publication, the editor of the paper had received harsh criticism from the authorities for publishing the piece and told "not to take this topic any further". Afterwards, A. F. Yeshtokin,

Second Secretary of the Central Committee of the Communist Party of the Soviet Union took control of Ivanov's investigation.

Ivanov also explained that, at the time, very little was known about UFOs or the effects of radiation, and public discussion of such topics was banned. Despite this, Ivanov continued to secretly investigate the fireballs and the Dyatlov Pass Incident. He communicated with scientists at the Ural Branch of the USSR Academy of Science and conducted extensive research on the clothing of the hikers as well as their internal injuries. He discovered that several items of clothing had an abnormal presence of radioactive dust. However, there could have been an innocent explanation for this: at the time, lamp wicks were commonly made of a ceramic gauze treated with radioactive thorium and would crumple to dust if damaged. Ivanov also questioned local people who might have witnessed fireballs or UFOS in the subpolar Urals on 17 February. One of them, A. Savkin, told him: "At 6:40 in the morning . . . a ball of bright white light appeared that [was] periodically enveloped in a cloud of white dense fog. Inside this cloud was a bright, luminous point, [like] a star. Moving towards the north direction, the ball was visible for 8–10 minutes."[4]

Ivanov concluded that "the role of UFOs in this tragedy was quite obvious". He believed the fireball had released radioactive energy, killing the skiers that had sustained internal injuries. "Someone needed to frighten or punish people, or show their strength, and they did this." He wrote how the rest of the skiers then carried their comrades away from the tent to be buried, but were themselves overcome by the bitter conditions. "This is how real people behave. We have something to take from the past, and how petty the behaviour of other people now seems, who cannot even overcome ordinary difficulties," he commented. Ivanov detailed how, after reporting his findings to his superior, A. F. Yeshtokin, he was ordered to classify everything, seal it up, hand it over, and forget about it. This was why Ivanov had remained quiet until 1990.

Many other possible explanations for the group's fate have since been put forward, ranging from the possible to the outlandish, spawned by the Soviet authorities' hasty conclusion of the original investigation. One is that the group had stumbled across something they shouldn't have, perhaps a government secret, and were killed to silence them. Another theory is that they were the accidental victims of a Soviet missile test. Some have even speculated that the hikers fell victim to alien predators or attack by a yeti. Those of a more down-to-earth turn of mind maintain that a natural disaster or some freak weather phenomenon could have been the cause.

The incident has also sparked suspicions of foul play. When the case was originally investigated, there was speculation that the indigenous Mansi people could have murdered the skiers for trespassing on sacred land. However, there was no evidence to corroborate these rumours. None of the skiers had sustained soft tissue damage from blows perpetrated by another person or a weapon. Moreover, the Mansi people were friendly to outsiders and no additional footprints were discovered leading away from the tent, other than those of the skiers. Conspiracy theories connecting the Mansi people have continued, however, one being that a Mansi shaman had confessed to putting a hex on the group for invading their holy site.

Theories of foul play continued, however. In 2014, the Discovery Channel produced a documentary titled *Russian Yeti: The Killer Lives* that postulated that the hikers had fled from their tent because they had encountered a yeti. According to Bigfoot Field Researchers

Organization curator Dr Jeffrey Meldrum: "Many, many hypotheses about what transpired and what happened to these people exist. Some have hung the yeti theory on the presence of footprints and that, when you look at the cameras, they found this single shot of a ghostly figure emerging from the treeline."[5] Critics of the documentary's assertion, however, say that the photograph in question shows an adult male human being and that Dubinina's tongue and eyes, far from being ripped out by a yeti, were either eaten by a scavenging animal or had decomposed, owing to the effects of the stream in which her body had lain for some time.

Some commentators considered that the group may have somehow been connected to the government. Yuri Kuntsevich, head of the Dyatlov Memory Public Fund, told the state-run TASS news agency in 2016 that he believed that some of the skiers were members of the KGB and that they were on a secret mission to "provide support for a technology-induced experiment".[6] He seemingly reached this conclusion because the skiers were carrying lightweight photographic equipment that he claimed was "completely typical of highly complex expeditions that require maximally alleviating their load". Kuntsevich suspected that the skiers were double agents who had been tasked by a Western agent named "The Mole" to photograph a secret Soviet missile test in the Ural mountains. However, they were captured and murdered. Those responsible then "moved the tent 1.5 kilometres [1 mile] to an impractical place. That was done by a mop-up team of soldiers; they had several helicopters".[7] According to Kuntsevich, only four of the skiers' ten rolls of film were recovered, as well as only three diaries when each skier had kept a diary during their trip. "All these factors confirm ties with the KGB: they were not simply hikers: they had been sent to the mountain pass on a special mission," stated Kuntsevich.

In his investigation, published in 2012 as *The Dyatlov Pass Incident,* Alexei Rakitin suggests that Zolotaryov, Kolevatov, and Krivonischenko were all members of the KGB on a secret mission. He concluded that they were supposed to meet with American agents and carry out a "controlled delivery", which included handing over samples of radioactive clothing. When handing over the clothing, it was allegedly Zolotaryov's role in the mission to photograph the American agents. The mission went awry when the American agents caught on and killed the skiers. This theory makes little sense, however. Why would a "controlled delivery" take place in the wilderness of the Ural mountains when it could have taken place in a city where the KGB agents would more easily blend in? His theory also does not satisfactorily explain the skiers' cause of death or the strange injuries that four of them sustained. According to Rakitin, however: "There can be only one conclusion –almost the entire group was evenly beaten."[8]

Whispers of a military cover-up stem from the fact that fragments of scrap metal were discovered in the area where the skiers were found. Some have speculated that the military were testing a new rocket or missile that may have malfunctioned and exploded, forcing the skiers to make a quick evacuation. According to a doctor who participated in the autopsies, only an explosion of some kind could have caused the sort of injuries that the four hikers had sustained. However, there is no record of rockets being fired around that time from either the Baikonur Cosmodrome spaceport or military bases in the Novaya Zemlya archipelago, both of which were in the vicinity of the group's last known camp.

The fireball sightings chronicled by Lev Ivanov in 1990 led some to believe that the Soviet army could have been testing parachute mines, an explosive that is dropped from an aircraft by a parachute that detonates 3 m (10 ft) from the ground. According to this theory, the group's tent would have been flattened by the blast, causing them to cut their way out. Shell-shocked from the explosion, the hikers could have staggered from the tent and died. As for the internal injuries, they could have been caused by falling debris.

Keith McCloskey, author of *Mountain of the Dead: The Dyatlov Pass Incident*, agrees that it is possible that the expedition accidentally stumbled across a military testing area and were either accidentally or deliberately killed by the Soviet military. Building on this supposition, Kizilov Gennadiy Ivanovich, a journalist from Yekaterinburg, also believed that the group was killed by the military and/or KGB after stumbling across something they shouldn't have. He asserted that the investigation at the scene was sloppy and, after examining related documents, had discovered "about forty signs of the presence in the area of the search of so-called outsiders", and that there was no way to be sure whether footprints at the scene had come from the group or from somebody else. He also speculated that, after killing the hikers, the military and/or KGB brought their bodies from the murder scene to the places where they were found and staged the incident. To support his supposition, he said that on 24 February, a search helicopter flew over the spot where the tent was later discovered, but saw no tent. However, the following day, another helicopter hovering overhead allegedly saw the tent with two corpses next to it. However, the next morning, when the tent was discovered by the search and rescue team on the ground, no bodies were found.[9]

Another popular theory is that the group's tent was engulfed by an avalanche and the group had to cut open the tent from the inside to escape. However, if an avalanche had occurred, then the scene inside the tent would have been in total disarray, yet many items were neatly arranged. In addition, the effects of an avalanche does not explain the injuries some of the skiers incurred or the others' lack of injuries. If the group had been hit with such force as to cause skull fractures and broken ribs, one of which pierced the heart, then it seems unlikely that only four of the skiers would have been affected. Finally, the pass was not an area prone to avalanches, and footprints indicated that the skiers had left the tent with ease; if they had suffered injuries while in the tent, it seems improbable they would have been able to walk at all let alone for any distance.

Donnie Eichar, author of *Dead Mountain: The Untold True Story of the Dyatlov Pass Incident* investigated the case for five years and blamed an intriguing phenomenon named a Kármán vortex street. The phenomenon was named after Theodore von Kármán, a Hungarian physicist, and is the result of a rare wind pattern that causes uneasiness, terror, and illness by producing infrasound, a low frequency that is below the limit of human hearing. In the 1960s, the scientist Vladimir Gavreau pioneered research into this strange phenomenon. He discovered it when his laboratory assistants started to complain of earache and queasiness. He deduced that microscopic air waves were projecting from a faulty fan. Although the sound could not be heard, it caused panic, fear, confusion, and sickness.

In 2003, an experiment was conducted in the UK whereby 700 people were exposed to music that had been mixed with infrasound waves. A quarter reported feeling anxiety, sorrow, uneasiness, and a strong pressure on the chest. According to Eichar, strong winds in the Ural mountains could have produced infrasound waves that caused the skiers to experience a range of illogical emotions. When wind flow is disrupted, the moving air can create a vortex that then travels away from the source. Eichar maintained that the group's tent was in the perfect location to feel the effects of minute air waves flowing down from the peak of a nearby mountain. A combination of high winds and the curvature of the mountain terrain could have conspired to produce infrasound waves. These might have caused the skiers to feel groundless fear and panic, leading them to flee their tent, ignoring the obvious dangers. By the time the group was far enough away from the effects of the infrasound waves, the skiers were unable to make their way back to the safety of their camp, and succumbed. Those who had sustained injury could have done so when they fell down the ravine where they were later discovered. The only flaw in Eichar's hypothesis is that there is no evidence that Kármán vortex street can cause people to act so irrationally. The group would have known that venturing out of their tent without the proper clothing and equipment was a virtual death sentence.

In February 2019, Russia's Prosecutor General's Office announced that it would be reopening the investigation into the Dyatlov Pass Incident to dispel the "growth of rumours". The investigation was moved from the regional branch of the Investigative Committee to the federal branch and focused on just three theories: a hurricane, an avalanche of mountain snow, and a type of avalanche known as a snow slab, whereby a slab of compacted snow slides over a weaker layer. The latter is a frequent cause of deaths in mountainous regions in winter. These possibilities had been whittled down from around 75 hypotheses, including a paranormal disaster and a government conspiracy. It was stressed that all conspiracy theories had been ruled out and that the government had played no part in the tragic deaths. "A large part of these 75 versions stem from conspiracy theories this or that way alleging that the entire incident was engineered by the authorities. It is absolutely out of the question, and we have proved that 15 theories explaining the hikers' deaths by secret activities of law enforcement agencies are ungrounded," declared Andrei Kuryakov, Chief of Justice Administration Oversight Directorate of the Sverdlovsk region prosecutor's office.[10]

However, the new investigation shed little light and did little to quell speculation. With so many peculiar elements involved in the mystery, it seems unlikely that belief in some kind of Soviet government cover-up or conspiracy will ever entirely disappear.

The Dyatlov Pass Incident has become one of Russia's best-known unsolved mysteries. What happened that night to force nine highly experienced skiers to rip open their tent and rush towards death? Despite all the efforts of modern-day science and technological advances, the crux of the mystery remains. It is a question that haunted the sole survivor, Yuri Yudin, until his death in 2013: "If I had a chance to ask God just one question, it would be, 'What really happened to my friends that night?'"[11]

The Abduction of Barney and Betty Hill

Over half a century ago, Barney and Betty Hill were driving through New Hampshire's White Mountains when they claimed that they were abducted by extraterrestrials. Their story attracted national attention and has inspired movies, TV shows, and best-selling books. The state of New Hampshire has even marked the spot where the abduction took place. Despite decades of investigation, speculation, and controversy, the alleged alien abduction of Barney and Betty Hill still defies logical explanation.

"Barney, stop the car and look! You've never seen anything like this in your life!"

Betty Hill

Barney and Betty's otherworldly adventure began on 19 September 1961. The couple was driving their 1957 Chevrolet Bel Air from Niagara Falls, where they had been enjoying a short vacation, to their home in Portsmouth, New Hampshire. Barney, 38, and Betty, 41, had only married in May the previous year, and their trip was something of a belated honeymoon. Both had been married before.

It was a warm autumn evening, the sky was clear, and the moon almost full. At around 10 pm, they were driving along the desolate, two-lane Route 3 near Lancaster, New Hampshire, when Betty spotted a bright light in the sky. She assumed that the light was a shooting star, while Barney said it was probably just an off-course satellite. "When I looked at it first, it didn't seem anything particularly unusual, except that we were fortunate enough to see a satellite," recollected Betty. "It had no doubt gone off its course and it seemed to be going along the curvature of the Earth. It looked like a star, in motion." However, Betty soon noticed that the bright object appeared to be following them, disappearing and then reappearing behind trees or a mountaintop, as they passed through Franconia Notch State Park.

The couple's dachshund, Delsey, was becoming agitated, so the couple decided to pull over and let her relieve herself while they took a short walk to stretch their legs. The object was still visible in the sky and Barney suggested that it could be an aeroplane, possibly a Piper Cub. However, it now appeared to be moving erratically and unpredictably. Barney suggested that the pilot could be having fun with them. Betty, however, wasn't convinced. She claimed that the object must be a UFO and that it was following them. They climbed back into their car and continued their journey. Betty continued to insist that the object was a UFO, while Barney dismissed her assertion. Betty's family had once claimed to have seen a UFO in Kingston, New Hampshire. Betty had believed them, but Barney was sceptical; he did not believe UFOs existed.

Continuing on their way, Barney and Betty rounded a curve near the Indian Head rock formation. Hovering around 24 to 30 m (80 to 100 ft) above them was a large, flat disc. "Barney, stop the car and look!" shouted Betty. "You've never seen anything like this in your life." Barney slammed on the brakes, bringing the car to a halt in the middle of the road. He grabbed his binoculars to get a closer look at the disc. He would later recall that, by this point, he was starting to feel afraid. He had no idea what the thing could be; unlike a plane or helicopter, it was totally silent.

Despite his fear, Barney felt an overpowering impulse to get closer to the object. He later recounted that the hovering disc was around 18 to 24 m (60 to 80 ft) in diameter with V-shaped wings with red lights on the tips. Across the front of the object was a double row of rectangular windows. Staring through his binoculars, he saw up to a dozen humanoid figures staring through the windows at him and Betty. The disc slowly began to descend. Barney rushed back to the car. Trembling with fear, he exclaimed to Betty that they needed to get out of there or they were going to be "captured".[1]

Barney and Betty accelerated down the highway. The UFO followed and swooped down directly above them. A strange buzzing and beeping sound began to emanate from the disc that appeared to bounce off the Hills' car. An odd tingling feeling passed through their bodies. "What's that? What's happening?" cried Betty. "I don't know . . . I don't know what it is," replied Barney.

What happened next is shrouded in mystery. The next thing they knew they were some 56 km (35 miles) south of Indian Head with no idea how they had got there.

When they finally reached home, Betty and Barney were puzzled to discover that Betty's dress was torn and stained with a pink substance, and that Barney's shoes were scuffed and his trousers stained. Furthermore, both their watches had stopped and neither of them had any memory of two hours of the drive.

On their car, they noticed several shiny spots. When, the following day, a compass was placed on one of them, its needle spun wildly, as if the normal magnetic field had been disrupted in some way.

The following day, Betty placed a call to the 100th Bomb Wing at Pease Air Force Base in Newington, New Hampshire, to report a UFO sighting. Both she and Barney described the object that they had seen in the sky. Barney omitted to mention the humanoid figures he had spotted in the craft's windows because he feared ridicule. Later that day, Major Paul W. Henderson phoned the Hills and questioned them about what they had seen. Betty wrote in her diary, "Major Henderson asked to speak with Barney, who was hesitating about talking on the phone. But, once he was on the phone, he was giving more information than I had. Later, Barney said he had done this, for Major Henderson did not seem to express any surprise or disbelief." Major Henderson reported the Hills' experience to the US Air Force's Project Blue Book, a government initiative set up in 1952 to study UFO sightings and decide whether they were a threat to national security: "On the night of 19 – 20 Sept. between 20/0001 and 20/0100 Mr and Mrs Hill were traveling south on Route 3 near Lincoln, New Hampshire, when they observed, through the windshield of their car, a strange object in the sky. They noticed it because of its shape and the intensity of its lighting as compared to the stars in the sky. The weather and the sky were clear at the time." Although the strange incident had taken place in the rural and desolate mountains of northern New Hampshire, Project Blue Book concluded that the object had the characteristics of an advertising searchlight.

In October 1961, Betty and Barney were interviewed by Walter N. Webb, a lecturer at the Hayden Planetarium in Boston, Massachusetts. Webb was also a scientific advisor to the National Investigations Committee on Aerial Phenomena (NICAP), and he occasionally investigated UFO reports from the New England area. Initially he was sceptical about interviewing the couple owing to the fact that Barney had reportedly seen movement inside the UFO and Webb typically disregarded such claims as fiction. Nevertheless, he sat down with the couple and questioned them both separately and together, fully expecting to be able to poke holes in their story. The interviews extended through lunch and into the evening. "I tried to make them slip up somewhere, and I couldn't; I simply couldn't. Theirs was an ironclad story," he said. Webb prepared his report for NICAP, concluding that "they were telling the truth, and the incident occurred exactly as reported except for some minor uncertainties and technicalities that must be tolerated in any such observation where human judgment is involved (i.e., exact time and length of visibility, apparent sizes of objects and occupants, distance and height of object etc.).”

In the following weeks and months, Betty and Barney suffered from nightmares, increasing anxiety, and irrational fears. Barney also experienced stress-induced health issues, including mysterious wart-like growths on his groin, high blood pressure, and an ulcer. Three years after their ordeal, they sought the help of Dr Benjamin Simon, a distinguished psychologist and neurologist.

During World War II, Dr Simon had been Chief of Neuropsychiatry and Executive Officer at Mason General Hospital, Washington, where he had successfully used hypnosis to treat psychiatric disorders among military personnel.[2] In particular, he used hypnosis to unlock what he called cases of “double amnesia”, caused by traumatic experiences. Dr Simon separately placed Betty and Barney under hypnosis, encouraging them to relive the events of the “missing” two hours, which had apparently been repressed by their conscious minds.

First, Barney was taken back to that evening in September. He slowly recalled climbing out of the car with his binoculars, determined to prove that Betty's UFO assertion was wrong. By this point, he had become annoyed by Betty's stubbornness over the nature of the object: “I say to myself: I believe Betty is trying to make me think this is a flying saucer . . .” Looking through his binoculars, Barney expected to see a satellite, or possibly a hovering helicopter. When he focused on the bright object in the sky, what he actually saw was a pancake-shaped object with “rows of windows” and “one huge light”. He remembered feeling scared and wanting the object to just go away. He then spotted eight to ten humanoid figures that he described as “somehow not human” looking out of the windows.

Their arms were going up and down as if they were controlling levers. "What do they want?" he wondered.

Barney recalled one of the aliens in particular. Dr Simon asked him whether this alien reminded him of anyone. Barney replied, "I think of a red-headed Irishman. I don't know why. I think I know why. Because Irish are usually hostile to Negroes [which was how he identified]." However, this alien appeared to be friendly, and even had a large grin on its round face. The aliens were wearing black leather outfits that reminded Barney of black-clad Nazi officers. All of a sudden, Barney was overcome with the fear that they were planning to abduct him and his wife. "I gotta get my gun! I'll shoot it down!" Barney, suddenly panic-stricken, shouted at Dr Simon.

Barney then told Dr Simon that he remembered being unaware of where Betty was at this time. Then he felt the leader of the aliens telepathically urging him to "stay there and just keep looking". According to Barney, the aliens' leader looked evil and had haunting, slanted eyes. Barney felt as though he was in a trance and couldn't move. He remembered pleading with God to give him the power to flee back to his car. Somehow he managed to do so, and he and Betty attempted to escape. By this point in the hypnosis session, Barney was completely hysterical. He had begged Dr Simon to wake him up twice already, but the doctor had refused: when a patient asks to be awoken, it is typically because they are about to experience a painful event, one so painful that they do not want to face it again, even while in a trance. Dr Simon believed that his tough stance would ultimately help Barney face – and deal with – whatever had traumatized him.

Barney next recalled that a group of aliens appeared before them on the road and helped him out of his car. He was so overcome with panic and fear that he could not open his eyes. He remembered being taken up a slight incline. Describing the aliens, he said, "They were by my side, and I had a funny feeling because I knew they were holding me, but I couldn't feel them . . . I felt floating, suspended." He recollected lying on something or being "inside something", but wasn't sure what because he did not want to open his eyes. When he eventually did so, he told Dr Simon that he appeared to be in a hospital operating room that was pale blue. As he lay on a table, he felt as though somebody was putting a cup around his groin and he felt a tug or pressure. In a later hypnosis session, Barney suggested that the aliens were taking a sperm sample from him.

When Dr Simon placed Betty under hypnosis, her account of being abducted eerily matched Barney's story. She recalled how, after they attempted to flee from the UFO, they came across "men standing in the highway". She described how these men approached the car in two groups; by this point, she had been overcome by a "kind of daze". One group led her from the car, while the other took Barney. "Don't be afraid. We're not going to harm you," one of the men said to Betty. She said that the men took them inside the UFO. She described walking up a long corridor and into a room, while Barney was taken into another room. "Another man comes in . . . I think he's a doctor . . . They push up the sleeve of my dress and they look at my arm . . . and then they turn my arm over, and they look at the underside . . . And they rub, they have a machine . . . it's something like a microscope, only a microscope with a big lens," said Betty. She described how they scraped her skin with something that looked similar to a letter opener and then placed the scrapings onto a piece of plastic.

Betty also remembered that they took swabs from inside her

mouth and plucked out several strands of her hair. One of the men then felt around her neck, behind her ears, under her chin, and around her collarbone, and then examined her feet. Another man cut off a piece of her fingernail and then ordered her to take off her dress. She complied and was then placed on a table and poked and prodded with needles. "It doesn't hurt at all," she told Dr Simon. Next, Betty remembered the aliens putting a needle into her navel and informing her that it was a pregnancy test. Betty told the doctor that when Barney was led out of the room where he had been examined, his eyes were closed. Towards the end of her hypnosis session, Betty recalled staying behind and arguing with the aliens' leader because she wanted to take a souvenir so that people would believe her. "I do wish I could have some proof of this, because it is the most unbelievable thing that ever happened," said Betty. While this was going on, a group of aliens took Barney and put him back in the car. During his hypnosis session, Barney had recalled that he was returned to the car before Betty. They also both remembered that, after getting back in the car, Betty asked, "Well, do you believe in flying saucers now?"

Initially Betty and Barney decided against going public with their story, fearing widespread ridicule. They worried that they would lose their jobs and status in their community. Up until now, the couple had enjoyed a simple, quiet life. Betty, who had graduated from the University of New Hampshire in 1958, was a social worker, and Barney was employed by the US Postal Service. They were an interracial couple – unusual at this time – and were politically active, involved in the National Association for the Advancement of Colored People (NAACP) and various literacy programmes. Barney had also been appointed to serve as an advisor to the US Commission on Civil Rights. The couple's niece, Kathleen Marden, recalled,

"I think it was difficult for Barney in some ways; he was afraid that they would become laughing stocks. He thought it would take away from the work they were trying to do."[3]

Betty and Barney were forced to go public in 1965 when a family friend leaked their story to a reporter for the now-defunct *Boston Evening Traveller*. The Hills' story was featured on the newspaper's front page in October 1965 and numerous other news outlets subsequently picked up the story, which soon began appearing in publications all over the world. The following year, the Hills' account was turned into a book by John G. Miller titled *The Interrupted Journey*, and in 1975 it was adapted as a TV movie, *The UFO Incident*, starring James Earl Jones and Estelle Parsons.

Betty and Barney's story is widely considered to be the very first documented and legitimate case of alien abduction. Sceptics and believers remain divided on what Betty and Barney Hill saw that night. The doubters maintain that Betty and Barney simply saw a star-like light that appeared to be following them. Out of fear, they turned off the main highway and travelled through narrow mountain roads, losing track of time.

One of the most prominent sceptics was Dr Benjamin Simon himself, whose sessions probing the couple's subconscious minds had yielded such remarkable results. In 1975, Dr Simon commented on Boston's WBZ radio's *Larry Glick Show* that the Hills' abduction claims were never truly about aliens or abduction, but instead were more about a black man's fears and a white woman's dreams. In the interview, he told listeners that hypnosis had revealed the "marked anxiety Barney had of being a black man in a white culture".[4] He explained that Barney, who had been married before, felt tremendous guilt for leaving his first marriage and deeply missed his sons. He went on to describe how marrying a white woman in the early

1960s – an era when interracial marriage was still illegal in some US states – had added to his deep-seated psychological problems. According to Dr Simon, Barney was a nervous wreck and whatever he saw that night had been intensified by his already existing "feeling of anxiety, feeling of being watched, feeling of danger". He suggested that it was Betty who believed in UFOs and that her subsequent nightmares had fuelled the dreamlike narrative of their abduction story. In short, Dr Simon suggested that the entire alien abduction story was simply the product of Betty's imagination.

Immediately following the couple's UFO encounter in 1961, Betty started to write down the nightmares that she had been having about being abducted by aliens. According to Dr Simon, the nightmares Betty detailed in her dream journal matched her and Barney's accounts while under hypnosis. When presented with this information, Betty was adamant that she had never shared her nightmares with Barney, but admitted that she had told others about them when Barney was nearby, possibly close enough to overhear her. During one of the hypnosis sessions, Dr Simon suggested this to Barney, but he was adamant that his memories of the abduction had not stemmed from Betty's nightmares. "No. She never told me that. I was lying on the table, and I felt them examining me," he insisted. "I am telling you what actually happened. At the time Betty was telling about her dream, I was very puzzled, because I never knew this happened . . ."

The Pulitzer Prize-winning astronomer Carl Sagan was among the Hills' debunkers, but nevertheless he still considered their claims to be noteworthy. He described their experience as "the first alien abduction story in the modern genre", and observed that it was the template for countless ensuing accounts of alien abductions. Sagan also speculated that the alien abduction claims from Betty and Barney had been a shared dream. Betty and Barney tried to sue Sagan, when "Encyclopedia Galactica", episode 12 of his *Cosmos* TV show (broadcast on 14 December 1980), cast their abduction in an unfavourable light. However, since Betty and Barney claimed that their story was fact as opposed to fiction, they couldn't trademark it.

For believers, however, there is one particular portion of the Hills' hypnosis sessions that gives an air of legitimacy to their claims. While hypnotized, Betty recalled that, before being returned to her car, she had asked one of the aliens where they had come from. She claimed that the alien told her that she would not recognize the area if he were to show her on a star chart, and that even if he did show her, she wouldn't remember. Betty insisted that she would and the alien showed Betty a constellation that he could see from his home planet. He pointed out heavy lines, which he had marked as trade routes, and broken lines, which he had marked as tracing various space expeditions. In 1964, Betty recreated the configuration of stars that the alien had shown her. At the time, astronomers were unable to identify the constellation. However, in 1969, the constellation that Betty sketched all those years ago was identified by amateur astronomer and UFO researcher Marjorie Fish as Zeta Reticuli.[5] Her opinion was given some weight by an article in the December 1974 edition of *Astronomy* magazine. It was not until the early 1990s that science, in the form of data from the European *Hipparcos* satellite that accurately measured hundreds of thousands of stars' distances from the Sun, disproved Marjorie Fish's interpretation of Betty Hill's star chart.

The Hills' niece, Kathleen Marden, 13 years old at the time of the abduction, was sceptical of the Hills' claims until, much later, she analysed tape recordings of the couple's hypnosis sessions. "Barney's description, though told from his own perspective, was nearly identical to Betty's," she said. "Each independently told Dr Simon that the men split into two groups of three and approached each side of the vehicle."

Marden spent 15 years investigating the Hills' accounts, and in 2007 she and co-author Stanton T. Friedman published the book *Captured: The Betty and Barney Hill UFO Experience*. During her investigations, Marden found that scientific analysis of the dress that Betty was wearing on the night of the alleged abduction revealed an anomalous biological substance. The dress had also sustained extensive damage to the zipper, hem, and lining that could not be explained. "I attempt to set the record straight. So much scepticism is based upon inaccurate information. I'm sceptical until I see evidence. So I think that it's a matter of informing people about the truth," said Marden.[6] She concluded that Betty and Barney had been abducted that night and that the event had been covered up by the US Air Force and other government agencies. She pointed to the fact that Project Blue Book had quickly dismissed what Betty and Barney had seen that night by suggesting that the UFO was an advertising searchlight. "It made no sense whatsoever, but that's what the Air Force wanted people to think," Marden commented in 2017.[7]

Marden also attempted to explain Barney's descriptions of the aliens themselves. When the statements he made under hypnosis were made public, many people suggested that Barney had simply been observing humans, possibly even military personnel. She asked the reader to remember that Dr Simon had told Barney to express all of his innermost thoughts and emotions. When he described feeling threatened by the alien who reminded him of an

Irishman, he was taken back to experiencing racial prejudice at the hands of the Irish. When he described the leader of the aliens as looking like a Nazi, he was taken back to World War II, when he was serving in the army.

After reluctantly going public with their story, Betty and Barney became staunch advocates of creating a legitimate outlet for people to discuss UFOs and alien abductions without fear of being mocked. Throughout the 1960s, they appeared on national talk shows, and Barney continued to wonder whether what he claimed he had seen during hypnosis was real or just a figment of his imagination. In 1967, they were confronted on television by a panel of esteemed scientists, including Carl Sagan. Barney was bluntly asked what exactly happened that night. "Ask Betty first," Barney replied, to which Betty responded, "I believe we were really captured."

Barney passed away suddenly from a cerebral haemorrhage in 1969 aged just 46. Betty, the more gregarious of the couple, became a celebrity on the UFO circuit and became known as the "First Lady of UFOs" and the "Grandmother of All Abductions". She travelled extensively and gave lectures on UFOs and extraterrestrials, before retiring in her seventies, complaining that the quest for knowledge about aliens had become tainted by commercialism. Since the Hills' experience, abduction claims had proliferated, and Betty claimed that people were making up false stories. "If you were to believe the numbers of people who are claiming [to have been abducted], it would figure out to [be] 3,000 to 5,000 abductions in the United States alone every night. There wouldn't be room for planes to fly."[8] She also lambasted the media, stating that they were perpetuating UFO fiction. In a 1997 interview with the Associated Press, she commented, "The media presented them [UFOs] as huge craft, all brightly lighted and flashing, but they are not. They are small, with dim lights, and many times they fly with no lights." Tom Elliot, the founder of Boston Paranormal Investigators, commented: "She felt her story was the only legitimate one."[9]

After a battle with lung cancer, Betty Hill passed away in 2004 at the age of 85. In 2011, a historical marker was erected by the state of New Hampshire at the Indian Head resort to commemorate the Betty and Barney Hill UFO encounter. It reads, "On the night of September 19–20, 1961, Portsmouth, N.H., couple Betty and Barney Hill experienced a close encounter with an unidentified flying object and two hours of 'lost' time while driving south on Rte. 3 near Lincoln. They filed an official Air Force Project Blue Book report of a brightly lit cigar-shaped craft the next day, but were not public with their story until it was leaked in the *Boston Traveller* in 1965. This was the first widely reported UFO abduction report in the United States."[10]

Betty and Barney Hills' alleged encounter with extraterrestrials changed their lives and, as the very first credible report of an alien abduction, UFO history. While many doubted – and still doubt – their claims, the Hills were adamant about what they had seen that night. "Don't be afraid," Betty once reassured the readership of the *Los Angeles Times*. "They don't hurt anybody. If they wanted to conquer us, they would."[11]

The Falcon Lake Incident

The Falcon Lake Incident remains Canada's best-documented and most famous UFO case. Several decades later, speculation is still rife over what occurred that day, when one man allegedly witnessed the landing of an extraterrestrial spacecraft near picturesque Falcon Lake – and suffered the consequences.

———————

"It's still one of the most important ones that's been researched."

Ed Marker, provincial director for the Mutual UFO Network (MUFON)

———————

In May 1967, Stefan Michalak was enjoying a long weekend away at Falcon Lake, Manitoba. Born in Poland in 1916, he enlisted in the Polish army just before the outbreak of World War II, and later joined the Polish Home Army in resistance operations against the Nazis. It was during this turbulent time that Stefan met Maria, his future wife. Maria was working with the Polish partisans as a courier, but in 1943 she and her two sisters were arrested by the Nazis and sent to Ravensbrück concentration camp.[1] All three were among the fortunate to survive until their liberation in 1945. Maria and Stefan were married the following year. By now, Stefan was serving with the resistance against the country's new Communist regime. He was forced to escape from Poland to Canada with help from the Allied occupation forces, leaving behind Maria and their two children, Ewa and Mark.[2]

Almost a decade later, Maria and Stefan reunited in Canada. Following the birth of a third child, Stan, the family settled in River Heights, Winnipeg. Stefan fully embraced the Canadian passion for the great outdoors. He developed a love for animals and birdwatching, but it was geology that became his number-one passion. Stefan frequently ventured out into the woodlands and rocky terrain of eastern Manitoba. His favourite spot was Falcon Lake, situated in the Whiteshell Provincial Park in southeastern Manitoba, approximately 75 km (47 miles) north of the US border. The area is widely known for its various mineral deposits and is a popular destination for hikers, fishermen, and amateur geologists. Stefan had successfully searched for quartz and silver there and even staked a few claims.

For May 1967's Victoria Day long weekend – a national holiday – Stefan decided to explore Falcon Lake for precious metals. He collected his tools, including a hammer, welding goggles, map, compass, paper, pencil, and enough food for the trip. He caught the bus to Manitoba and checked into a motel on the south side of the Trans-Canada Highway, as he had done many times before.[3] The following morning, Saturday, 20 May, Stefan got up at 5:30am and crossed the road into Whiteshell Provincial Park. It was a bright and sunny day without a cloud in the sky. He wended his way through the park's pine trees and climbed over rock formations, heading toward Falcon Lake. Around noon, wearing welding goggles and protective gloves, Stefan was chipping away near a vein of quartz along the Precambrian Shield when he was startled by a gaggle of geese nearby that suddenly began honking in unison.[4] "Something had obviously frightened them far more than my presence earlier in the morning when they gave out a mild protest," Stefan recalled.

Glancing up at the sky, Stefan saw two cigar-shaped objects with a reddish glow and "humps" on them. He estimated that the objects were around 10.7 m (35 ft) in diameter and 3.7 to 4.6 m (12 to 15 ft) in height. They were hovering around 46 m (150 ft) away and were eerily silent. According to Stefan, one of the objects began to descend, landing on a flat rock nearby. As it descended,

Stefan realized that it was more disc-shaped than cigar-shaped. The other object remained hovering in the air for several minutes. As it began to ascend, Stefan saw that its colour began to change from a reddish glow to an orange shade before turning grey. Once in the clouds, Stefan said its colour changed once again – to bright orange. The craft that had landed on the rock also changed colour "from red to grey-red to light grey and then to the colour of hot stainless steel, with a golden glow around it". Stefan noted that the craft looked as though it had an opening on the top from which a brilliant purple light was issuing. This light was so intense it hurt his eyes, and he donned his welding goggles. Stefan assumed that the craft must be some US military experiment. He looked for any markings associated with the US Air Force, but saw none. He then sat watching the object for half an hour, sketching it on his notepad.

Once his sketch was complete, Stefan decided to approach the object. As he drew near, the air became noticeably warm and he could smell sulphur. He heard the whirring sound of motors and a hissing sound, which he described as sounding like "air had been sucked into the interior of the craft". Stefan spotted a door open on one side with bright lights emanating from it. He also heard faint voices. "They sounded like humans, although somewhat muffled by the sounds of the motor and the rush of air that was continuously coming out from somewhere inside," he recalled.[5] Stefan described two different voices, one of which appeared to be significantly higher in pitch than the other. Still convinced that the craft was some kind of experimental military craft, he felt a surge of excitement at witnessing something no ordinary citizen had seen before. Wondering if, perhaps, something had gone wrong with the craft, Stefan decided to offer mechanical assistance. "Okay, Yankee boys, having trouble?" he called out to the voices. "Come

on out and we'll see what we can do about it."[6] The voices immediately went quiet. Perplexed, Stefan wondered if maybe the
occupants didn't speak English. He cautiously called out in Russian,
German, Italian, French, and Ukrainian, but received no response.[7]

Standing right next to the craft, Stefan noticed that it appeared
to be made of some unnaturally smooth metal substance with no
apparent seams or joints. The walls of the craft were extremely thick,
around 51 cm (20 in), and highly polished. Stefan was an industrial
mechanic with extensive knowledge of automotive machinery,
welding, and metalwork, yet he had never seen anything quite like
this vehicle before. He took off his goggles and peered in through
the open door. "The inside was a maze of lights," he recalled. "Direct
beams running in horizontal and diagonal paths and a series of
flashing lights, it seemed to me, were working in a random fashion,
with no particular order or sequence." As he stepped back from the
door, two panels rapidly slid over the aperture and a third dropped
over them from above, completely closing it off. Stefan noticed a
small, screen-like pattern on the side of the craft that looked like
some kind of vent, with slits of around 0.5 cm (a quarter of an inch)
in diameter. He placed his hand on the craft and felt an intense heat
that melted the fingertips of his glove. Moments later, the object
began to turn counter-clockwise and, before Stefan could react, he
was struck in the chest by a blast of gas or air that pushed him to the
ground and set his shirt and cap on fire. He managed to rip them
both off as the craft took off. It hovered above the treetops and
changed colour and shape, turning back into the cigar-like form
Stefan had first observed. The UFO then flew away, leaving a sudden
rush of air in its wake.

Immediately afterwards, Stefan felt disoriented and nauseated
from whatever it was that had shot out of the craft and engulfed

him. He picked up his belongings. The needle of his compass was whirling around as if controlled by some kind of magnetic force. A crushing headache overcame him and he broke out in a cold sweat as he stumbled back through the woods, stopping on occasion to vomit. "I knew that something totally unnatural had happened to me and, apparently, it was having an adverse effect on my physiology," he said. As Stefan was making his way back to his motel, he saw a Royal Canadian Mounted Police (RCMP) constable. He gave the officer an account of what he had just witnessed and warned him not to come any closer, for fear that he might have been exposed to radiation. "Sorry, but I have duties to perform here," replied the disinterested RCMP constable. Stefan was astounded. "He, apparently, did not believe a word I told him," said Stefan. "The constable left me with my sickness and disappointment."

Stefan eventually returned to his motel and was on the bus back to Winnipeg by evening. After he arrived home, his son Mark drove him to Misericordia Health Centre, Winnipeg, where he was treated for second- and third-degree burns to his chest and stomach. When a doctor asked him what had caused his injuries, Stefan said he had been "hit by exhaust coming out of an airplane".

Stefan worried that he didn't have the linguistic ability in English to make his fantastic story sound convincing. At the time, Stefan's other son, Stan, was just 9 years old, but even at that age he knew that something was wrong with his father. "I recall seeing him in bed. He didn't look good at all. He looked pale, haggard," he said. Stan was allowed to see his father for only a couple of minutes on the day that he returned home, but one thing stuck in his memory: "When I walked into the bedroom, there was a huge stink in the room, like a real horrible aroma of sulphur and burnt motor. It was all around and it was coming out of his pores. It was bad."

For weeks after the incident, Stefan suffered from diarrhoea, headaches, blackouts, and weight loss. In a weight journal, he documented that in the space of just one week, he lost 10 kg (22 lb). His burns turned into raised sores that appeared in a grid-like pattern – an ugly reminder of his traumatic experience.

Before moving to Canada from Poland, Stefan had been a military policeman. He had great respect for authority and a strong sense of moral responsibility. If he saw something unusual, Stefan believed it was his duty to inform the authorities of what he had seen. More than anything, he wanted somebody to explain to him what he had witnessed and what had happened to him. If it was something dangerous, he wanted people to be prepared.

Local newspapers caught wind of the incident and ran numerous articles about Stefan and his encounter. Most of these reports were sceptical. "I didn't realize, as I recounted the events of the previous day, that this was the beginning of a long series of questions and harassment by the press, radio, television, the air force, and various authorities," he said.

Reporters and journalists descended on the family's bungalow and camped out on their lawn, hoping to catch a comment from Stefan. They even followed Stan to school, questioning him about what his father had seen. For Stan, school was no release from the harassment. He was bullied by classmates who mocked his father. "It just flipped our lives over. It took several years before it finally died down," recalled Stan.

The media circus that followed the incident also led to numerous Ufologists and scientists flocking to the scene. "It was very big," recalled Ed Marker, provincial director for the Mutual UFO Network (MUFON). "It's still one of the most important ones that's been researched."

Canadian and United States government officials were called in to investigate Stefan's claims. The Royal Canadian Mounted Police (RCMP), the Royal Canadian Air Force (RCAF), and the Canada Army Personnel Research Office (CAPRO) scrutinized the scene and discovered a circle around 4.6 m (15 ft) in diameter that was devoid of the moss and vegetation growing in the surrounding area. They also noticed that pine needles and leaves on the ground had been scorched.[8] They retrieved several items, including Stefan's glove, shirt, and some tools that he had dropped when blasted by the gas or air. Soil samples were collected and sent off for analysis at an RCMP lab, along with the items collected. Although the lab was unable to determine what had caused the burns on various items, they discovered that both them and the soil were highly radioactive. An RCAF report noted that "there are certain facts, such as Mr Michalak's illness and burns and the very evident circle remaining at the site, which are unexplainable".[9]

In June 1967, New Democratic Party (NDP) member of parliament Ed Schreyer (who would later go on to become Governor General of Canada) stood up in the House of Commons and inquired about UFO investigations and Stefan's claims. "I had felt obligated to ask a question – it happened in my riding [district]," he said. "Plus, I was intrigued that someone seemed so genuinely convinced he had seen something inexplicable." The question was taken by Prime Minster Lester Pearson, and a few days later he offered Schreyer a chance to look through the government files on the matter "from which a few pages have simply been removed". Schreyer refused, stating that if he looked through the files, he would need to keep the contents confidential and that this would put him in a problematic position. Reassured that there was no significant danger to the country, he let the matter drop. Shortly afterwards, defence minister Leo Cadieux announced that it wasn't the intention of the Department of National Defence to make public the report of the sighting.

The following year, Stefan visited the Mayo Clinic in Rochester, Minnesota, and paid for an examination out of his own pocket, since his Canadian medical insurance would not cover it. The mysterious burn marks kept showing up on his chest and he was having recurring blackouts. Twelve separate doctors investigated Stefan and his ailments, and they concluded that his burns were caused by an unidentified chemical substance that his body had absorbed under extreme pressure.[10] They could not determine, however, what was causing his other health issues. During an examination at the Whiteshell Nuclear Research Establishment, Stefan was given a whole-body count that measured radioactivity within his body. It showed nothing above normal background readings.

During the immediate period following Stefan's Falcon Lake encounter, his blood lymphocyte (a type of white blood cell) count had dropped from 25 to 16 percent. Some commentators have suggested that Stefan may have been affected by high doses of radiation; but if so, his blood lymphocyte count would have varied far more substantially. However, according to Dr Horace Dudley, a radiologist at the University of Southern Mississippi, Stefan's "nausea and vomiting followed by diarrhoea and loss of weight is a classical picture of severe whole-body exposure to radiation with x- or gamma-rays. I would guess that Mr Michalak received on the order of 100–200 roentgens [a unit of ionizing radiation]. It is very fortunate that this dose of radiation only lasted a very short time or he would certainly have received a lethal dose." Other scientists have also speculated that the raised burns on Stefan's chest were radiation burns.

In addition to being physically examined, Stefan was sent to a psychiatrist, who determined that "this is a fellow who's very pragmatic, very down to earth, pardon the pun, and does not make up stories".

Trying to make sense of what he saw that afternoon, Stefan wrote a pamphlet about his experiences, in which he states: "Up until the time and the events I am about to describe I had no special interests in 'flying saucers' and other strange phenomena one hears about time and again. Maybe they are real, maybe not, but I had never been seriously concerned about them. Not until May 20, 1967, when I, perhaps as nobody else – or at least very few – came in such a close contact with one of those strange objects commonly called UFOs."

He ended the pamphlet by not blaming the craft for the injuries he had sustained. "The burns and suffering I had endured were not caused by any aggressive moves of the craft of its occupants . . . If I had stayed farther away from the craft I would not have been burned or suffered in any other way."

In the aftermath of the Falcon Lake Incident, Stefan's claims were frequently dismissed as an elaborate and calculated hoax. Just a few weeks after his encounter, Stefan had trouble finding the location where it had taken place, prompting suggestions that the reason he couldn't find it was because he had made the whole thing up. The area, however, was off the grid and Stefan hadn't been following a particular route; he had just been walking through the woods and rocks searching for minerals. Another puzzling aspect of the incident was that it had all taken place within view of a forest ranger tower. The ranger on duty that afternoon said that he had not seen any strange craft in the vicinity and had not seen any of the bright lights that Stefan described in such great detail.

Squadron Leader Paul Bissky of the Royal Canadian Air Force – who was investigating the case – bluntly asked Stefan if he had been drinking any alcohol on the day of his UFO encounter that might have caused him to hallucinate the entire incident. The idea that Stefan had hallucinated the sighting made little sense owing to the fact that Stefan's injuries and subsequent ailments were very real. According to Bissky, however, a potential alternative scenario was that Stefan had burned himself on a barbecue grill while drunk. At one point during the investigation, Stewart Hunt, the head of the Radiation Protection Division of the Canadian Department of National Health and Welfare, even speculated that Stefan could have planted the landing site with commercially produced radium and had Stefan's home and place of employment searched to check for radiation. No radiation was found. Despite his attempt to poke holes in Stefan's story, Hunt was forced to concede that the incident was "unexplainable".

Stefan himself never claimed that he had had a close encounter with extraterrestrials and continued to believe that the UFO he had seen was a secret military craft. Moreover, in the wake of going public with his story, the publicity surrounding the case tormented him and his family. "If you asked him what it was he saw, he would describe it in intimate detail but would never say, 'Oh, it was definitely extraterrestrials,' because there was no evidence to prove that," said Stan. Whether Stefan truly believed this or only claimed to believe this out of fear of further ridicule is open to question. "If it's a hoax, it has enough complications to make it one of the best on record," said Ufologist Chris Rutkowski. "It is even better than Roswell, because with that one, the government denies anything happened . . ."

Many observers latched onto the secret military craft theory.

Department of National Defence engineer Palmiro Campagna concluded that Stefan had witnessed an experimental craft originally developed by Avro Canada. The Avro Canada VZ-9 Avrocar was a VTOL (Vertical Take-Off and Landing) aircraft designed by Avro Canada in the late 1950s on behalf of the US military. The Avrocar was a large silver disc, around 8 m (26 ft) in diameter and 1.6 m (5 ft) tall. It had US military markings on the top of its hull. In addition, it also had pads enabling it to land on any surface. When the Avrocar took off, it blew exhaust out of its rim, and once in the air it resembled a flying saucer. However, the Avrocar had been a complete failure, proving too unstable to fly higher than 1 m (3 ft) or much faster than 50 kmph (30 mph). The US military spent more than $7 million on the project before cancelling it in September 1959.[11]

While Stefan himself may have been a nonbeliever, many Ufologists believe that the Falcon Lake Incident was a genuine "close encounter of the second kind" – broadly defined as a UFO event in which the witness experiences a physical effect and physical impressions, such as scorched vegetation, are left on the ground.

As an adult, Stan became a big aviation fan and extensively researched aviation technology. "There was nothing even close to [what my father saw] in the works anywhere at that time," he later said. Local resident Bob Firth is a firm believer that Stefan saw something unexplainable. Years later, Firth – who was 14 years old at the time of the incident – corroborated what Stefan had witnessed. Firth had been at the beach on the south side of Falcon Lake when he and his three friends saw something to the north of the lake, moving westwards. He described how he looked on as an object "just jumped across the sky". Firth and his friends joked, "It's a bird, it's a plane, it's a flying saucer!" At the time, Firth didn't think too much of it, until news of the Falcon Lake Incident spread. "In my mind, I can still see it . . . Something crossed the sky and disappeared," he said.

In fact, after Stefan's experience was documented in the media, several people reported UFO sightings around the same time in that area. On 19 May 1967, residents in Lockport, near Winnipeg, reported a UFO with a "glowing ring of heat" moving at "indescribable speed". Two nights later, three people at Eleanor Lake in Whiteshell Provincial Park reported seeing a "round, reddish, glowing object at treetop level". On 25 May, two men watched a "large, cigar-shaped object travel across the horizon at a tremendous speed". On the same night, two witnesses saw "two very brilliant stars in close proximity to each other" over Winnipeg. Years later, another man reported a UFO encounter that took place around "the same time as Michalak" in the park's West Hawk Lake. He had been walking to Caddy Lake along the highway between it and West Hawk Lake when he saw a large, disc-shaped object gliding above the trees before vanishing. The man's sketch of the UFO was similar to the craft that Stefan had drawn. Then in 1992, another witness came forward to claim that she and her daughter had spotted a UFO on the highway near Falcon Lake over the same weekend as Stefan. She described it as a "perfectly flying saucer" that appeared to be spinning counter-clockwise. She, too, had sketched the craft and it was eerily similar to Stefan's drawing.

The Falcon Lake Incident marked the end of Stefan's prospecting hobby. He no longer wanted to venture out into the wilderness in search of precious metals – it reminded him too much of the incident. Stefan regretted sharing his experience for the rest of his life. Up to that point, he had always trusted the authorities and held them in high regard. However, so many members of the police and air force had disregarded his claims and considered him a liar that, in the aftermath of the incident, his trust was completely shattered. "I never should have said a word," he often said, up until his death, at the age of 83, in 1999.

In 2018, the Royal Canadian Mint commemorated the Falcon Lake Incident with a special commemorative $20 coin. "I was very surprised, frankly," said Stan. "They called me out of the blue."[12] The team behind the idea for the coin felt that the incident was a classic moment in Canadian history that they wanted to celebrate. "Everyone is sort of fascinated by this subject matter and we thought it would make a really interesting coin design," said product manager Erica Maga. One side of the coin carries a standard engraving of the Queen, but the other side displays a full-colour depiction of the moment that the craft lifted off the ground, with Stefan lying on the ground with his arm outstretched. Falcon Lake and the forest can be seen in the background behind Stefan, and the coin even glows in the dark. "I feel very privileged they're doing it. If my dad was still around, he would be floored," said Stan. "And if my mother was still here, she would say everything has a reason. Everything is connected. You do something here and there will be repercussions."[13]

The Isdal Woman

In November 1970, the badly burned body of a woman was discovered in an isolated, ice-filled valley in Norway. Despite numerous attempts, investigators have failed to crack the case, which was described by one investigator as "riddle upon riddle".[1] The mysterious death of the still-unidentified "Isdal Woman" has intrigued investigators for decades.

"This was during the Cold War,
and there were definitely a lot of spies
in Norway, including Russian spies."

Gunnar Staalesen, crime writer

Isdalen ("ice valley" in Norwegian), is situated some 19 km (12 miles) outside Bergen, Norway. While popular with local walkers, its inaccessibility attracts few tourists. Imposingly picturesque, this remote area is known locally as the Valley of Death. It earned this sinister nickname in medieval times because of its reputation as a notorious suicide spot. The valley has also been the scene of many accidental tragedies, when hikers, lost in fog, have fallen to their deaths.

On the afternoon of 29 November 1970, Professor Sund and his two daughters were hiking along Isdalen's scree slopes. Low clouds were drifting over the valley and it was a brisk 5°C (41°F).[2] Suddenly, the elder daughter spotted the body of a woman lying on her back between some boulders, a short distance from the path. Professor Sund told her to wait with her younger sister while he went to investigate. The woman's body had been set on fire. Her arms were outstretched, in a distinctive, pugilistic attitude – a position typical of bodies that have been burned. There were extensive burn marks on her face and torso. The damage to her face was so severe that her features could not be discerned. Fearful that a killer could be lurking among the tall trees surrounding them, the family swiftly hiked back down the valley to report their horrific discovery to the police.

Bergen police soon arrived on the scene, armed with metal detectors and assisted by sniffer dogs. Carl Halvor, one of the first officers to arrive, recalled in 2016, "The first thing we notice is the stench . . .,"[3] implying that the body had been there some time. The police cordoned off the area, and by late afternoon the desolate valley was teeming with investigators trawling through rocks and vegetation, searching for clues. Several objects were found at the scene: jewellery; a woman's watch; some Fenemal sleeping tablets; the remains of a pair of rubber-soled, lace-up boots of a type commonly worn by Norwegian women; two melted bottles that smelled like petrol; a silver spoon; part of a half bottle of the State Liquor Store's Kloster Liqueur; and a broken umbrella. The watch and jewellery were not on the woman's person but appeared to have been arranged around her body. "It looked like there had been some kind of ceremony," observed forensic investigator Tormod Bønes.

The deceased woman was 1.64 m (5 ft 4½ in) tall, with long, brownish-black hair. She had a small, round face with brown eyes and small ears. Her age was estimated at between 25 and 40 years old. Her body was transported to the Gades Institute of Pathology at Haukeland University Hospital for a cause of death to be determined.

The autopsy and toxicology report concluded that the woman had died from a combination of the barbiturate Fenemal, a prescription drug, and carbon-monoxide poisoning. She had ingested more than 50 tablets in several doses in the hours leading up to her death. Many of the pills had not yet dissolved into her bloodstream before she died. Smoke particles in her lungs indicated that she had still been alive when she was set on fire. According to the police report, the woman had "been stained by a brief but intense fire". The pathologist's report added that injuries inflicted by the fire were also a contributing cause of death. It also noted that there was bruising to the woman's neck and face, which could have been caused by a blow or a fall.

Adding to the mystery, a portion of the woman's fingerprints had been sanded away and all labels had been cut from her clothes and scraped off the bottles found at the scene.

It quickly dawned on the local police force that this wasn't going to be an easy case, and the following day they asked for assistance from the National Criminal Investigation Service (Kripos) in Oslo. When they were unable to identify her, the woman became known as number "134/70" at the Gades Institute. To the public, however, she soon became "the Isdal Woman".

The first lead in the case came three days later, when investigators discovered two large unclaimed suitcases at the left-luggage office at Bergen train station. They had been checked in on 23 November. Inside, police discovered a notepad with a single handwritten entry that appeared to be in some kind of code; German and Norwegian money in the form of notes; and Belgian, Swiss, and British money in the form of coins. They also found some expensive-looking clothing, several wigs, a comb, a hairbrush, some teaspoons, spectacles with no corrective lenses, and a tube of eczema cream. On one lens of the spectacles was a partial fingerprint that matched the Isdal Woman, so at least it was clear that the suitcases had belonged to her.

Instead of helping to provide some answers, however, the contents of the suitcases only raised more questions about the woman's identity. Once again, identifying labels had been removed, including the patient and doctor details from the tube of eczema cream. Whoever had done this had been so meticulous that the labels had even been rubbed off the comb and hairbrush. The fingerprint found on the spectacles was sent to the Criminal Police Centre in Oslo and run through their fingerprint register. However, this yielded no results.

One item, however, did have an identifying feature. It was a shopping bag with the name "Oscar Rørtvedt's Footwear Store" inscribed on the front. Investigators located the store in Stavanger and spoke to the store-owner's 22-year-old son, Rolf Rørtvedt. He informed investigators that he remembered the unidentified woman, correctly describing her as being of medium height with long dark hair and dark eyes, and a roundish face. "She was a customer who took up space, asked a lot of questions, and spent a long time making up her mind," he recalled. "Her English was poor, and I remember a certain peculiar smell." She had come into the store several weeks before and purchased a pair of blue rubber boots. He showed investigators the brand of boots that the woman had purchased and they recognized them as similar to the boots found beside the Isdal Woman's body. Years later, Rørtvedt commented that, when garlic became a common ingredient in European cookery, he recognized the smell immediately as the odour that had emanated from the woman in his father's store. "In 1970, no one smelled like garlic – now, everybody does," he stated.

Confident that the Isdal Woman had been in Stavanger in the weeks leading up to her death, the police went from hotel to hotel asking staff whether they could remember a guest matching her description. A receptionist at the Hotel St Svithun was able to connect the Isdal Woman to a female guest who had recently stayed a night at the hotel. She described the woman as "dark-haired, golden skin, wide hips without being fat, speaks poor English". Checking through the registration cards, the hotel receptionist finally put a name to the woman: Finella Lorch from Belgium. It seemed like a major break in the case. The following day, the headline in Stavanger's *VG* newspaper read, "Sensational Solution Today?" However, that glimmer of hope soon enough faded when Bergen police checked the registrations of hotels in Bergen and could not find the name "Finella Lorch".

Investigators analysed the woman's handwriting in the notepad found inside the suitcase and continued to inquire about her in hotels throughout Norway. They eventually discovered that the woman travelled from town to town in Norway, staying in numerous hotels in the six months leading up to her death. Each time, she used a new alias and investigators found at least seven of them: Claudia Tielt, Vera Jarle, Alexia Zarna-Merchez, Claudia Nielsen, Genevieve Lancier, Vera Schlosseneck, and Elisabeth Leenhouwfr.

In addition, most of these aliases were supported by fake passports and a distinctive signature. During each hotel check-in, the woman claimed to be from Belgium, but after checking with Belgian police, investigators found out that each identity – and passport – was false; they could trace no Belgian citizen with any of those names. Even more peculiar, if the woman stayed in a hotel more than one night, she would always request to change her room and would often rearrange the furniture. If she were booked into a room with a balcony, she always requested a move. Staff at these hotels recollected that she wore wigs and could speak a number of different languages, adding that she spoke broken English with an accent.

Memories of the woman were hazy, but most witnesses described her as "confident", "quiet", "sexy", and as a woman "with an agenda". Witnesses who met her in Bergen recalled that she looked smart and sophisticated. Alvhild Rangnes, a 21-year-old waitress who was working in the dining room at the Scandic Neptun hotel in Bergen, recalled that when the Isdal Woman strolled into the dining room on her own, she was impressed by her confidence and expensive-looking clothes. She looked comfortable and had a proud posture. A woman dining alone was a rare occurrence back then, and Rangnes remembered that the woman looked as though she was used to travelling alone. "I remember I whispered to my colleague that I hoped I could adopt this woman's style as an adult," she said. From the glamorous image the Isdal Woman presented in the dining room, Rangnes could not picture her hiking in the bleak Isdalen valley. According to Frank Ove Sivertsen, who was working as a hotel bellboy in 1970, she was "the kind of woman we hardly ever saw".[4]

Investigators trawled through missing persons reports but were unable to find anyone matching the mysterious woman's appearance. They eventually cracked the coded entry in her notepad and determined that it was a record of the woman's many trips around Europe. She had recently visited Paris, Hamburg, and Basel. They also discovered that she had travelled from Paris to Stavanger and Trondheim, before returning to Stavanger and then finally heading to Bergen, fated to be her final destination. She had travelled from Trondheim on the Braathens SAFE Airline, and taken the hydrofoil between Stavanger and Bergen using the names E. Velding and L. Selling. Investigator Carl Halvor wondered, "What was she doing in those places? Why did she go there? And why did she want to conceal both her identity and travelling route by using these codes?"

Another seeming break in the case came shortly afterwards when the autopsy report noted that ten of the Isdal Woman's teeth had gold crowns, and the majority of these crowns were preformed, which meant that they were premade. The investigation called in

Professor Gisle Bang, who determined that the type of crowns on the Isdal Woman's teeth were not used in Scandinavia. He said they would be more common in "the Orient and in some parts of southern and central Europe". This information, combined with the fact that she had travelled from Paris to Stavanger, led investigators to speculate that the woman might have been French. Over the next few years, Professor Bang sent photographs of the woman's dental work to dental journals in various countries, hoping that somebody somewhere could identify where it might have been done. Unfortunately, the journals' experts were unable to pinpoint a precise location where the woman had undergone these procedures.

The bizarre case garnered extensive media coverage. Many early reports speculated that the Isdal Woman was a foreign spy who had almost certainly been murdered. The Cold War with the Soviet Union was ongoing and Norway was a NATO country with a 196-km (122-mile) border with Russia. Bergen was a strategic naval port, and there was a collective fear that Soviet forces could potentially launch an attack from the sea.[5] It was common knowledge that spies were operating in the country. "This was during the Cold War, and there were definitely a lot of spies in Norway, including Russian spies," observed Gunnar Staalesen, a Bergen-based crime author.

The rumour that the Isdal Woman was some kind of foreign agent circulated widely and, in a bid to calm public fears, the police held a press conference. "No, I think I can safely say that there are no grounds for espionage. I count it as completely out of the ordinary," declared Criminal Commissioner Oskar Hordnes. Sceptics questioned why a field agent would agree to meet somebody in such a remote location.

However, it later transpired that, around the same time as

Commissioner Hordnes was speaking to the press, a telegram from the Norwegian Defence Security Department (NORDSD) suggested that the Isdal Woman was associated in some way with the Penguin missile program, a top-secret collaboration between the Norwegian armed forces and the country's weapons industry. The telegram was labelled "Secret" and read: "Woman found dead in Isdalen probably observed Tananger in November while tests with Penguin were conducted."

Fisherman Berthon Rott, from the town of Tananger, just 10 km (6 miles) south of Stavanger, had informed the military that he had noticed a woman who could have been the Isdal Woman on the quays, where naval vessels were regularly moored. This woman had stood out from the crowd. "She was nicely dressed. You don't usually go that way on a fishing pier," he said. Rott claimed he saw the woman talking to "an officer" – presumably a naval officer – near motor torpedo boats that were playing an important role in the Penguin weapons program. Each boat carried a Penguin missile, which employed state-of-the-art infrared technology to target enemy warships. These boats, and in particular their Penguin missiles, were thus of great interest to the secret services of unfriendly countries. "They wanted to know how the missile worked, and how to deceive it," said Henry Kjell Johansen, one of the leaders of the Penguin program.[6]

Ørnulf Tofte, Assistant Chief of Police and head of counter-intelligence in the Police Surveillance Agency, had been sent from Oslo to Bergen to assist in the Isdal Woman case. During his investigation, he was never made aware of her possible connection with the Penguin missile program. He also said that he considered this claim very unlikely, believing that Soviet agents would employ more subtle and sophisticated methods to monitor the testing of new NATO weapons. "If they sent someone, they would probably have done so from the Soviet embassy in Oslo. Or sent some Russian fishing boats to the area. I don't think they would use a woman like her," he said.

When the "Iron Curtain" finally fell in 1991, none of the pseudonyms the Isdal Woman had used were found in the archives of the former spy services of Poland, the Czech Republic, Bulgaria, Romania, or East Germany. However, it is unknown whether any details of her identity reside in the files of the Russian Federal Security Service (FSB), which succeeded the Soviet Union's KGB.

In his book *The Woman in the Isdalen*, author Dennis Aske considers a theory that the Isdal Woman was a high-class sex worker. He suggests that this could be the reason she travelled so extensively and checked in to so many hotels.[7] Aske also mentions the police's description of underwear found in her suitcase, with its emphasis on the "brassiere's bowls, lace, cassettes, and a small bow". He suggested that the underwear had come from Beate Uhse, a shop in Germany that sold "sex products".[8] However, unbeknown to Aske, this theory was considered by police back in 1970 and quickly ruled out. The majority of the hotels she had stayed in forbade prostitution and all of the witnesses who came into contact with the Isdal Woman saw her on her own; she did not bring anybody up to her room and she dined and shopped alone.[9] Moreover, why would a client lure the Isdal Woman to the isolated area where she died and go to such extreme lengths to conceal her identity? When a sex worker is murdered, it is typically during a sudden fit of rage and the crime scene did not fit this scenario.

Perhaps for lack of any other obvious solution, or to calm public fears, several investigators eventually concluded that the Isdal Woman had committed suicide. They noted how difficult it would have been for someone to force another person to swallow such a large amount of Fenemal tablets. Bergen Chief of Police Asbjørn Bryhn said he believed that, in the grip of some form of mania, she had opted to end her life. One possible suicide scenario is that she hiked up to the remote location, drank the bottle of liquor found with her body, started the fire to burn her belongings and then took the final dose of Fenemal. As the drugs and alcohol took effect and before she lost consciousness, she may have thrown herself, or fallen, into the fire in a final bid to protect her identity.

Other investigators strongly disagree with the suicide theory, Carl Halvor among them. "If someone wanted to take their life out of the fact that they were sick, had problems, other reasons or whatever it might be, it is so unnatural to do it that way."[10] Knut Haavik, a crime reporter who investigated the case, also refuted the suicide hypothesis. "Personally, I'm totally convinced that this was a murder. She had various identities, she operated with codes, she wore wigs, she travelled from town to town, and switched hotels after a few days. This is what police call conspiratory behavior." Those who believe she was murdered also say that the remote location where she was found, combined with the brutal method of her death, make it seem extremely unlikely that she ended her own life.

Three years after the death of the Isdal Woman, on 21 July 1973, Israeli Mossad agents assassinated Achmed Bochiki in Lillehammer, Norway. They mistook the harmless waiter for Ali Hassan Salameh, leader of the Black September Palestinian militant group. The Isdal Woman investigation team questioned the four agents responsible while they were behind bars, but none of them recognized her or any of the aliases she had used.[11]

In May 2017, a DNA profile of the unidentified woman was compiled in a bid to finally crack the case. At the time of her death,

DNA technology had not yet been developed. However, the Norwegian Institute of Public Health in Oslo was now able to isolate the Isdal Woman's DNA from tissue samples. "What is new is that we have finally been able to create a DNA profile. The aim of sending it out now is that if she is reported missing and there is DNA from relatives in the database then we will get a match," said Maj Nordskaug of Kripos. The sample was sent to the Institute of Forensic Medicine at the University of Innsbruck. Analysis revealed that the Isdal Woman was of European, but not Scandinavian, origin. Scientists were able to narrow her birthplace down even further with isotope analysis, which looked at the chemical composition of strontium and oxygen absorbed in her teeth enamel as her teeth were forming. These substances settle in the enamel when drinking and eating, and the level of them can indicate where a person may have grown up. The results indicated that, during her formative years, the Isdal Woman had possibly moved from Southern Germany to France during World War II.[12] This analysis meant that future investigation into her identity could focus on these, admittedly large, areas.

The following year, another break in the case came when experts at the Forensic Medicine Agency at the Karolinski Institute in Stockholm examined the Isdal Woman's teeth and concluded that she was closer to 40 years old. Scientists had used a more modern method of analysis, known as carbon-14 analysis. This was linked to atomic bomb blasts. Between 1955 and 1963, thousands of nuclear bombs had been tested in the open air, causing a spike in the amount of carbon in the atmosphere. In 1963, the Nuclear Test Ban Treaty made this illegal. In future, nuclear weapons could only be exploded underground. When carbon is in the air, it settles in the enamel of a child's teeth as they are forming; once formed, the teeth do not absorb any more carbon. Because of this, people whose teeth formed after 1955 typically carry an extra "annual signature" in their tooth enamel. When the Isdal Woman's teeth were examined using carbon-14 analysis, it was determined that she had no increased carbon, meaning that her teeth must have been fully formed by 1955, making her approximately 10 or 12 years old by then. "There were no traces of the test blasts. So I can say with 100 percent certainty that she was born before 1944," said Kanar Alkass, a researcher at the Forensic Medicine Agency. In addition to the carbon-14 analysis, scientists also analysed the Isdal Woman's teeth using the racemization method. This used chemical analysis of the dentin in her teeth to calculate her age. The results estimated that she was born in 1930 or possibly a few years later, confirming that she was around 36 to 40 years old when she died.

In June 2019, a BBC World Service report provided a new possible insight into the mystery: the testimony of a former local man, Ketil Kversoy. He did not tell his story to police at the time for fear of ridicule. While walking on the slopes of the Isdal valley on a Sunday afternoon in November 1970, he recalled encountering a dark-haired woman. She was being followed by two men. "When she looked at me, I felt that she started to say something, but she didn't, and then she looked behind her and saw these men. I'm sure she knew they were going after her."

The Isdal Woman was given a Catholic funeral at Møllendal chapel in Bergen on 5 February 1971. Many of the officers who had tried so hard to identify her were in attendance. Her coffin – which was adorned with tulips and carnations – was lowered into the ground in the cemetery outside the chapel. There was no tombstone and there was no name. She was buried in a zinc coffin that will not decompose; therefore, if she is ever identified, her family can rebury her in her home country.

Photographs documenting the funeral remain stored at the Bergen police department in hopes that one day she will finally be identified and her family can be presented with them. To this day, the true identity of the Isdal Woman remains an enigma. The case is tinged with sadness, not only because of a life lost but also because her killer, or killers, may very well have evaded justice for decades.

The D. B. Cooper Hijacking

In November 1971, a suave-looking businessman hijacked an airliner, demanded $200,000, and then parachuted over Washington state, never to be seen again. He became the subject of poems and songs, the inspiration for television characters, and even entered the annals of crime as a legend alongside the likes of Bonnie & Clyde and Jesse James. The case remains the only unsolved air piracy case in history.

———————————

"I have a bomb in my briefcase.
I will use it if necessary . . ."

The man known as D. B. Cooper

———————————

The saga of D. B. Cooper began on a miserably wet and windy afternoon on 24 November 1971, when a man approached the flight counter at Portland International Airport. He had dark hair and a medium complexion, was between 1.7 and 1.8 m (5 ft 10 in to 6 ft) tall, weighed around 77 to 82 kg (170 to 181 lb) and was in his mid-to-late 40s. He was well dressed, wearing a business suit and raincoat and carrying a black suitcase that he checked in as hand luggage. He was unremarkable in every respect – just another airport visitor. The airline employee who attended him later recollected that the man's behaviour appeared perfectly normal as he booked himself a one-way ticket on Northwest Orient Airlines' Flight 305 that afternoon for Seattle, Washington, giving the name "Dan Cooper". He subsequently became known as "D. B. Cooper" after a wire service report erroneously referred to him this way.

The Boeing 727-100 departed Portland on time at 2:50 pm with Cooper sitting in seat 18C. There were only 36 passengers on board – less than a third of the plane's capacity. Once the plane was airborne, Cooper ordered a bourbon and soda and lit up a Raleigh filter-tipped cigarette (separate smoking sections on jetliners were not introduced until 1973; a smoking ban not introduced until late 1980s)[1].

Shortly after take-off, Cooper handed a note to flight attendant Florence Schaffner. Assuming the note was simply Cooper's phone number, Schaffner stuffed it into her pocket without reading it. She was used to unwanted attention from male passengers. "I thought he was trying to hustle me," she later said. Cooper then leaned forward and whispered, "Miss, you better look at that note. I have a bomb."[2] The note read, "I have a bomb in my briefcase. I will use it if necessary. I want you to sit next to me. You are being hijacked."[3]

Cooper slowly opened his briefcase, revealing a mass of wires and red-coloured sticks. "All I've got to do is touch the end of this wire to the terminal," he told Schaffner. He then ordered her to write down his demands: $200,000 in unmarked bills (more than $1 million today), four parachutes, and a truck waiting at Seattle-Tacoma (Sea-Tac) International Airport to refuel the aircraft. He said that if his demands were met, he would release all the passengers unharmed. If not, he would blow up the plane. Schaffner took the note and scurried off to the plane's cockpit where the pilot, William Scott, immediately contacted Sea-Tac air control. They contacted Seattle Police and the FBI, who in turn called Donald Nyrop, President of Northwest Orient Airlines. Nyrop contacted the pilot and instructed him to cooperate with Cooper and inform him that the company would pay the ransom.

Meanwhile, Cooper asked Schaffner to tell the pilot that he wasn't allowed to land at Sea-Tac until all the money was collected and the parachutes were ready. Cooper ordered another flight attendant, Tina Mucklow, to sit beside him. She later described him as being extremely polite, but occasionally impatient.

On the ground, the FBI began to gather the ransom from banks in the Seattle area. While the notes were unmarked, most were minted in 1969, in a series beginning with an L. Furthermore, the

FBI ran the bills through a Recordak machine, which created a microfilm of each one, capturing their serial numbers. The money was easy enough to collect, but the FBI had some difficulty finding four suitable parachutes. Initially, they planned to source military parachutes from McChord Field Air Force Base in Pierce County, Washington. However, Cooper demanded civilian sports parachutes, which allow for a much slower landing speed and are steerable. Eventually, Seattle police managed to track down suitable parachutes from a skydiving school in Issaquah, Washington.

When the aircraft landed at Sea-Tac Airport, the passengers and two flight attendants disembarked, leaving just Cooper, Mucklow, William Scott the pilot, first officer Bill Rataczak, and the flight engineer H. E. Anderson on board. Cooper ordered the pilot to taxi the plane to a secluded area and told him to dim the cabin lights to deter any police snipers. Cooper waited on board while the money and parachutes were delivered by a single Northwest Orient employee, who was ordered to drive up to the front door of the aircraft, where he was met by Mucklow. While the aeroplane was refuelling, Cooper detailed his flight plan to the remaining crew. He wanted the pilot to head towards Mexico City at the minimum speed possible and flying no higher than 3,048 m (10,000 ft). He also ordered the captain to fly with the landing gear down and the flaps lowered 15 degrees. The co-pilot, Bill Rataczak, informed Cooper that the plane's range was limited to approximately 1,610 km (1,000 miles) under his specified flight configuration. This meant that they could not get as far as Mexico without refuelling. Cooper, the pilot, and the co-pilot decided to fly to Reno, Nevada; refuel; and then head to Mexico City. "Let's get this show on the road," Cooper announced. The aircraft was back in the air at 7:40 pm. Unbeknown to Cooper, McChord Air

Force Base had sent a jet fighter, a jet trainer, and a cargo plane with parachutists aboard to shadow the flight.

The weather worsened and the 727 was soon flying through the night sky in a severe rainstorm. After approximately 20 minutes, Cooper ordered Mucklow to the cockpit. As she complied, she turned around to see Cooper putting on his parachute. He had cut the cords from one of the other parachutes to secure the bag of ransom money to his waist. At 8:13 pm, a warning light in the cockpit indicated that the aircraft's rear airstair had been unlatched. Over the intercom, the pilot asked if there was anything the crew could do to help. "No!" Cooper replied. That was the last they heard from him. Moments later, there was a change in air pressure, indicating that the rear airstair was open. The crew thought that Cooper had jumped from the aeroplane, but decided to take no chances and continued to Reno.

The lowered rear airstair scraped the runway and sparks flew as the plane landed. The crew then discovered that Cooper was gone. Nobody – including the crews in the following aircraft – had seen a thing. Cooper and his cash had literally disappeared into thin air, plummeting to earth in the dark. All Cooper had left behind were eight cigarette ends, a thin black tie with a mother-of-pearl tie clip, and two of the four parachutes. The authorities later pinpointed Woodland, Washington, as the most likely place that Cooper had landed. Lewis River runs through Woodland, and the surrounding country is peppered with deep ravines and dense forests. Even experienced hunters are regularly lost there.

The quaint town was rapidly transformed into a bustling command post for legions of FBI agents, police officers, and soldiers from Fort Lewis, Washington. A search party for the "very cool" hijacker – according to Fredericksburg's *Free Lance-Star* newspaper – was assembled right away. Assisted by planes, military and privately owned helicopters, Jeeps, and tracking dogs, the authorities set about exploring one of the nation's most remote forests, looking for the mysterious hijacker, or for any clues that might reveal what had happened to him.

The FBI announced that Cooper must have been "either an experienced jumper or crazy" to have pulled off such a dangerous stunt. He was wearing a light business suit and street shoes when he had parachuted into the pitch darkness of a thunderstorm. The wind strength at the time was 322 kph (200 mph) and the temperature -4°C (25°F). "Up looked like down to him. He had no visual reference. He couldn't have possibly known where he was," said FBI agent Ralph Himmelsbach.[4]

The FBI was working on the theory that Cooper was probably hiding in dense undergrowth and that he had most likely sustained, at the very least, a broken leg from the jump. However, freshly fallen, thick snow made searching for him almost impossible. After a week, assuming that Cooper must have died, the search was abandoned. The FBI believed they were simply looking for a body and a bag of money, and further investigation on the ground would have to wait until the spring thaw. In late March 1972, 300 soldiers duly combed the thawing terrain for almost three weeks. Once again, no body, no money, and no parachute were found. The FBI released the ransom serial numbers to financial institutions, hoping that somebody somewhere might have come into contact with the mysterious hijacker.

Eight years later, on 10 February 1980, 8-year-old Brian Ingram made a remarkable discovery. While playing on a beach along the Columbia River, approximately 14.5 km (9 miles) from Vancouver, he came upon three packets of cash, totalling $5,800. The notes' serial numbers exactly matched those of the ransom. Early reports said that the packets of money were scattered near each other and covered with sand. However, Brian's mother stated that the packets were together and had not been covered up.

Commentators speculated that Cooper had crash-landed into the Columbia River and that his body had become wedged in one of its many creeks. There was much debate as to how the money came to be there and for how long. The FBI believed that the cash had not been lying on the beach since 1971 because the elastic bands securing the packets had not disintegrated. The area had been dredged in 1974 and no money had been found then. Further-more, the packets were lying above clay deposits that had been deposited on the shore by the dredging. "High water lifted that money out," remarked local fisherman Sid Tipper. FBI operatives dug up the entire beach, but found no more cash or other evidence of Cooper's possible fate. Over the subsequent years, private divers painstakingly searched the Columbia River, but to no avail.

The baffling case initiated one of the longest and most exhaustive investigations in FBI history. In the immediate aftermath, reports concerning the elusive D. B. Cooper spread across the nation. While most people lambasted the hijacker, there were some – lawmen included – that commended him for his courage and intelligence. "If he took the trouble to plan this thing out so thoroughly, well, good luck to him," said one sheriff. "You can't help but admire the guy," said another FBI agent, who was a member of the initial search team.[5] Agent Himmelsbach, however, was not impressed with the cult-like following Cooper amassed, referring to him as "a stupid, desperate rascal who endangered many lives".

In 2000, there was a brief glimmer of hope that Cooper could be identified when the FBI announced that they had managed to extract DNA from the cigarette ends found on the plane. Seven years later, they announced that they had managed to get a partial DNA sample from the tie, but they couldn't be sure if the DNA was from Cooper or from somebody else. Meanwhile, the DNA samples from the cigarettes had inexplicably vanished.

Over the years, a plethora of theories have been advanced as to Cooper's identity and whether he could have survived his perilous parachute jump. The most common view is that he either died on impact, or from the harsh climatic conditions he subsequently encountered. The area near where Cooper had jumped was just 8 to 16 km (5 to 10 miles) from Interstate 5, a busy road. "I still think he perished, but you have to keep an open mind," commented Himmelsbach.

It was evident that Cooper had extensive knowledge of the 727 aircraft, of the Seattle area, and of airport procedure. He knew the correct terminology for equipment and knew exactly how long it should take the plane to refuel. He also knew that McChord Air Force Base would have available parachutes and that the rear airstair of the plane would lower in flight far enough to allow somebody to clear the plane if jumping from it. Furthermore, when the plane took off the second time, he ordered the pilot to fly at just 3,048 m (10,000 ft) with its landing gear in position and to lower the flaps 15 degrees to slow the aircraft down. Mucklow also said that Cooper knew exactly how to put on a parachute.

Between 1971 and 2016, the FBI processed over a thousand "serious suspects". From publicity seekers, such as Jack Coffelt, who claimed to be Cooper in the hope that he could sell his story, to deathbed confessions, like that of Duane Weber, who told his wife "I am Dan Cooper". Some have been more plausible than others, and many have been ruled out by the FBI. One outlandish theory even suggests that Cooper survived the jump but didn't survive an encounter with the legendary Sasquatch in Washington's dense woods.

One of the favourite suspects was Richard Floyd McCoy, a former Sunday-school teacher who perpetrated a 1972 "copycat" hijacking. On April 7, 1972, McCoy boarded United Airlines' Flight 855 in Denver. Once in the air, he claimed that he had a bomb on his person. He demanded four parachutes and $500,000, which was delivered to San Francisco International Airport. He jumped from the aircraft over Provo, Utah. However, he left behind a magazine covered in his fingerprints. He was tracked down and apprehended two days later and sentenced to 45 years in prison. Two years later, McCoy escaped from Lewisburg Federal Penitentiary and was killed by police officers in a shootout. Due to the striking similarities in the two hijacking cases, he was a lead suspect for numerous years. Bernie Rhodes, a former probation and parole officer for the District of Utah, and Russell P. Calame, a former FBI special agent in charge of the Utah State Bureau of Investigation, presented this theory in their 1991 book *D. B. Cooper: The Real McCoy*. However, the FBI later announced that he was not a suspect owing to significant differences between him and the description of D. B. Cooper. Nevertheless, McCoy remains a leading contender among numerous would-be sleuths.

Marla Cooper was "thoroughly convinced" that her "odd uncle", Lynn Doyle Cooper, was the hijacker. In a 2011 interview with ABC News, she recollected how, over the Thanksgiving holiday in 1971 (when she was just eight years old), her uncle was visiting her grandmother's house in Sisters, Oregon. During the visit, he alluded to "plotting something underhanded". Marla claimed that her uncle Lynn informed her that he was going turkey hunting. When he returned from his trip, he was badly injured, and she overheard him telling her father that he had hijacked an aeroplane. Marla also heard him saying: "Our money problems are over. We just need to go back and get the money." Marla said that she had never really given too much consideration to this strange memory until her mother briefly mentioned the incident before her death two years earlier. The comments her mother made jogged Marla's memory and she decided to research the D. B. Cooper case. "Over the next few days, I was just flooded with memories of what happened," she said.[6] DNA testing failed to link Lynn to the tie that Cooper had left behind on the plane. However, Special Agent Fred Gutt cautioned that the test did not necessarily rule him out as a suspect because it was impossible to determine whether the DNA on the tie was that of the hijacker or of somebody else who had handled the tie.[7]

One of the more peculiar suspects to emerge was John List, who, on 9 November 1971, murdered his wife, mother, and three children in their home in Westfield, New Jersey. After slaughtering his family, List went on the run. He had planned the murders so meticulously that the bodies of his victims were not discovered for a month. Fifteen days after the List murders, Cooper hijacked the Northwest Airlines Boeing 727. List wasn't apprehended until 1989. He had assumed a new identity and created a new life for himself in Virginia; his new wife and friends were completely unaware of his real identity. Soon after his arrest, rumours circulated that he was Cooper. "D. B. Cooper? That's about as ridiculous as anything I've ever heard," said New Jersey Police Chief James Moran, who had spent much of his career tracking down List. According to Himmelsbach, however, List "fits the profile, the description", adding, "He's the kind of guy with nothing to lose." In 1971, List was 41 years old, while Cooper was estimated to be around 48.[8] Ultimately, there was no conclusive evidence to indicate that List was Cooper, and the FBI subsequently confirmed that they did not consider him a genuine suspect.

A long-time skydiving and aviation enthusiast named Ted Mayfield was also suspected of being the elusive hijacker. Mayfield had served in the 101st Airborne Division during the Vietnam War, where he learned to skydive. In the immediate aftermath of the 1971 hijacking, he met with FBI agents who were seeking advice on whether it was possible to jump out of a Boeing 727. While Mayfield was a skydiving expert, he said that he wasn't sure. However, when he discovered that the rear airstair could be lowered mid-flight, he concluded that it would be possible. Agent Himmelsbach dismissed the notion that Mayfield was the hijacker early on in the case, but, years later, Daniel Dvorak and Matthew Mysers, two amateur researchers, proposed him as a suspect once more and stated that they had found circumstantial evidence to prove he was Cooper. However, when they inquired where he was between 2 pm and 8:15 pm on the day of the hijacking, Mayfield retorted that he was at parachute school in the city of Donald, Oregon, during the day, had a dinner engagement that night, and that several people could vouch for his whereabouts. "They said Cooper was tall and slender. I told them I'm not tall and slender. I'm 4 inches too short and 40 pounds too heavy."[9]

In 1995, Mayfield was charged with two counts of criminally negligent homicide in connection with two skydiving deaths at his skydiving business, Sheridan Sky Sports. He agreed to plead guilty after the charges were reduced to second-degree manslaughter and served five months in prison. He passed away in 2015 after sustaining a fatal injury while attempting to manually turn over the propeller of a plane at Sheridan Airport.

For years, Lyle Christiansen of Morris, Minnesota, waged a campaign to prove that his brother, Kenneth, could have been the infamous Cooper. Kenneth Christiansen was a former US Army paratrooper and flight attendant on Northwest Orient who at one time had lived in Bonney Lake, Washington. Lyle had watched an episode of the popular *Unsolved Mysteries* TV show on the Cooper case (first broadcast in 1988) and, when the FBI sketch of Cooper appeared on screen, was immediately struck by its resemblance to his brother. As his conviction grew, Lyle attempted to persuade the filmmaker Nora Ephron to make a movie based on his suspicions.

From the beginning, the FBI was distinctly unenthusiastic about Lyle's claims, as were some of Lyle's neighbours. One of them, Julia Bowen, recalled that Kenneth had a lot of money and was always generous with it before he passed away from cancer in 1994, but she could not imagine him carrying out such a crime.[10] In 2007, the FBI commented that Christiansen wasn't a viable suspect because he weighed just 68 kg (150 lb) and was only 1.7m (5 ft 8 in) tall.

Yet another suspect in a long line was Barbara Dayton, the first woman in Washington to have a sex-change operation. Dayton was born Bobby Dayton in 1926 and had gender-reassignment surgery in December 1969. She lived in West Seattle and had experience as a recreational pilot. She served in the US Merchant Marines and with the US Army during World War II. Following her discharge, she worked with explosives in the construction industry. She hoped to become a pilot, but was unable to obtain a commercial pilot's licence. According to her friend Ron Forman, she disguised herself as a man to carry out the hijacking as a way to get back at the airline industry and the Federal Aviation Administration (FAA). According to her family, she never spent the $200,000 because she hid it in a cistern in Woodburn, Oregon, near where D. B. Cooper landed.

Dayton's family later withdrew their claims for fear that she could be prosecuted for the crime. Forman suggested that the small amount of money that was discovered on the Columbia River shore could have been planted by Dayton to spark interest in the case. The FBI, however, said that Dayton did not match the description of Cooper. Flight attendant Mucklow confirmed that she had sat so close to Cooper that she would have noticed if he were a woman.[11]

A further suspect came to light in 2016 when the History channel ran a documentary titled *D. B. Cooper: Case Closed?* It was the work of Tom Colbert, who spent five years researching the Cooper case with a team of 40 investigators. The programme suggested that Cooper was Robert W. Rackstraw, a 72-year-old Vietnam War veteran and paratrooper then living in Southern California. In 1969, Rackstraw was stationed at Fort Rucker, Alabama, for helicopter and fixed-wing flight training before being deployed in Vietnam. He returned to Fort Rucker in 1971 and was detained for domestic assault. A later military investigation charged Rackstraw with falsifying college records and lying about his rank and medals. In due course he was forced to resign from the army for claiming he was a Green Beret and for fabricating five campaign ribbons and five Purple Hearts. Rackstraw's troubles with the law were only beginning: In 1978, he was acquitted of murdering his stepfather before faking his own death. He was later convicted of grand theft and passing bad cheques. Colbert noted that Rackstraw had been mentioned in the original FBI files. Colbert also believed that Cooper was working for the CIA, who had concealed his identity. Colbert's team's analysis of handwriting samples and DNA evidence did not rule out Rackstraw as the hijacker. Rackstraw himself had made teasing

The Falcon Lake Incident

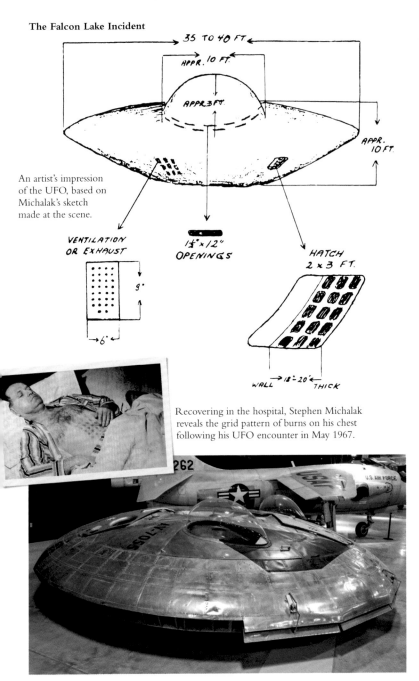

35 TO 40 FT

APPR. 10 FT.

APPR 3 FT.

APPR. 10 FT.

An artist's impression of the UFO, based on Michalak's sketch made at the scene.

VENTILATION OR EXHAUST

9"

6"

1½" x 12" OPENINGS

HATCH 2 x 3 FT.

WALL

18" - 20" THICK

Recovering in the hospital, Stephen Michalak reveals the grid pattern of burns on his chest following his UFO encounter in May 1967.

A possible explanation for the Falcon Lake UFO: the experimental Avro Canada VZ-9AV Avrocar, shown here in the National Museum of the United States Air Force.

A wooden cross marks the spot where the body of the Isdal Woman was discovered in Isdalen Valley, locally nicknamed "The Valley of Death".

The picturesque, snow-covered woods and valleys near the city of Bergen, Norway – the scene of a baffling mystery in November 1970.

The D. B. Cooper Hijacking

The Northwest Orient Airlines ticket purchased by "Dan Cooper" on November 24, 1971.

FBI sketches of the hijacker who, thanks to a news report error, became known as D. B. Cooper.

FBI agents dig in the sand on the Columbia River's north shore, searching for the hijacker's cash.

The hijacked Boeing 727 refueling at Seattle–Tacoma International Airport, November 25, 1971.

The Lord Lucan Case

Nanny Sandra Rivett, who – it is believed – Lord Lucan mistook for his wife and murdered.

Following the murder, a policeman guards the entrance to the family home in Belgravia, London.

Wing Commander Ken Wallis joins the police hunt for Lord Lucan flying his autogyro – which also featured in the James Bond film *You Only Live Twice*.

Police on horseback and with dogs search Peacehaven Golf Course, Newhaven.

Lord Lucan and his
future wife Veronica
photographed shortly
after the announcement
of their engagement on
October 14, 1963.

The Rendlesham Forest Incident

The scene of alleged UFO activity in December 1980 – Rendlesham Forest, Suffolk, England.

A board in Rendlesham Forest supplies information for tourists eager to walk the forest's UFO Trail.

Skinwalker Ranch

A view overlooking Uintah Basin, Utah, homelands of the Ute people and also the location of Skinwalker Ranch.

Navajo petroglyphs in Uintah County prompted speculation that the curse of a skin-walker – a witch that can transform or possess an animal – could have been placed on the ranch.

A poster for *Skinwalker Ranch*, a 2013 film dramatizing the eerie events alleged to have taken place there.

A spectacular view of the
Hale-Bopp comet – a
possible explanation for
the 1997 Phoenix Lights
UFO sightings.

The Northrop–Grumman B-2
Spirit stealth bomber came
into service in the same year as
the Phoenix Lights Incident,
prompting speculation that
witnesses could have mistaken
it for a UFO.

comments to the media about the D. B. Cooper case. "I wouldn't discount myself . . .,"[12] he once said to a reporter who asked him if he was the notorious hijacker. When questioned during the documentary, Rackstraw refused to either confirm or deny that he was Cooper; he would only say that the evidence the programme had accumulated was intriguing. Colbert later wrote a book about his investigations titled *The Last Master Outlaw.*

Colbert's investigation discovered another clue that potentially linked Rackstraw to the case. In December 1971, the *New York Times*, the *Los Angeles Times*, the *Washington Post,* and the *Seattle Times* received a letter allegedly from Cooper himself. Although there had been numerous hoax letters in the past, the FBI was particularly interested in this one because it revealed details not publicly released. The letter also contained a series of seemingly random numbers, which the FBI was unable to decipher. Colbert hired Rick Sherwood, a code breaker for the United States Army Security Agency (ASA) during the Vietnam War, to examine the numbers. According to Sherwood, Rackstraw would have had the same army "basic cryptology" training as him. Sherwood found possible ciphers in the numbers that identified Rackstraw's Vietnam military units: the 371st Radio Research Unit, the 11th General Support Company, and the ASA.

Back in 1979, the FBI had looked into the possibility that Rackstraw might be D. B. Cooper, but ruled him out because the hijacker was estimated to be in his forties and, in 1971, Rackstraw was only 28 years old. Nevertheless, the FBI conclusion quite evidently hadn't quashed theories that Rackstraw was the culprit.[13] According to Colbert, the FBI refused to look at the evidence he and his team accumulated because they "don't want to admit that a group of volunteer investigators solved a high-profile case that its G-men couldn't".[14] If Colbert was anticipating a deathbed confession from Rackstraw, he was sorely disappointed. Rackstraw passed away from natural causes in 2019.

The previous year, another suspect came to light: Walter "Walt" Reca. According to Carl Laurin, author of *D. B. Cooper & Me: A Criminal, a Spy, My Best Friend*, Cooper was none other than his best friend, Reca, a former military paratrooper and intelligence operative. The two men had met in the 1950s, bonded over their mutual love of skydiving, and remained friends over the years. "My best friend, Walter, was a daredevil. He was determined, he was fearless, he was tough as nails and had a temper, and he carried more pain than any man I've ever known," said Laurin. He began suspecting that Reca was Cooper, but when he questioned him, Reca was evasive and refused to answer. In the years leading up to Reca's death in 2014, he allegedly gave Laurin his story under the proviso that Laurin would not reveal his true identity until after his death. Laurin would listen to Reca over the phone and then send him written notes of what he had said. However, Reca never signed this "confession".

Reca's niece, Lisa Story, said that she thought it possible that her uncle was Cooper. She recalled that, after the date of the hijacking, Reca had spent his money at places that routinely dealt with large cash deposits, perhaps to avoid detection. He had also put a down payment on a house, purchased furniture and a car, as well as deposited money in a safety-deposit box at a Canadian bank. Story suggested that the reason Reca was never investigated by the FBI could have been because, after the hijacking, the government had employed him as a covert intelligence operative.

Those who support the Reca theory point to the testimony of truck driver Jeff Osiadacz. He was driving his truck near the rural resort of Cle Elum, Washington, on the night of the hijacking when he spotted a man walking along the road. It was raining heavily and Osiadacz assumed that the man's car had broken down and he was walking to get help. Osiadacz had no room for a passenger in his cab, so he continued on to the Teanaway Junction Café, near Cle Elum. While drinking a coffee, Osiadacz saw the same man enter the café, looking like a "drowned rat". His hair was dark, slicked back from the rain, and he had a raincoat folded under his arm. The man sat next to Osiadacz. At one point he called "a friend" on a pay phone and asked Osiadacz if he could give this friend directions to the café. Osiadacz complied and didn't ask the mysterious stranger any "stupid questions", judging from the man's appearance that he might be mentally ill. The man thanked him, paid for his coffee, and left. It was not until the following day that Osiadacz found out about the hijacking. He said that the original FBI sketches looked nothing like the man he had encountered, but when contacted by Laurin, he said that the man looked exactly like Reca.[15]

In 2016, the FBI announced that they were no longer actively investigating the Cooper hijacking and that resources dedicated to the case were now being allocated elsewhere. During the 45-year investigation, the FBI had exhaustively reviewed every credible lead, interviewed all identified witnesses, and collected all available evidence. In those 45 years, FBI agents had come and gone, applying the latest investigative technology techniques. The case evidence is preserved at FBI Headquarters in Washington, DC. It includes Cooper's boarding pass, a few deteriorated banknotes, Cooper's tie, and the pink parachute Cooper left on the plane after using its strings to secure the ransom to his body.

Along with other aircraft hijackings in the 1960s and 1970s, the

D. B. Cooper case played its part in transforming airline travel; metal detectors, luggage-screening machines, and handheld body scanners would soon become commonplace at major airports around the world. Cooper's final contribution to aircraft design was the Cooper vane, a latching device on Boeing 727s that prevented the rear airstair from being lowered mid-flight.

The story of D. B. Cooper has gained a flourishing cult following. Some consider him a suave gentleman thief, comparable to Robin Hood, claiming that he harmed nobody and successfully outwitted a large corporation, Northwest Orient Airlines. They like to believe that he survived the parachute jump and, after committing the "perfect crime", resumed his place in society. "People don't want me to find him," said former FBI agent Richard Tosaw, who conducted his own private search for Cooper. "They don't want to hear that D. B. Cooper failed."[16] As well as numerous books, the case inspired a 1981 feature film, *The Pursuit of D. B. Cooper*, starring Robert Duvall in the title role. Each year, the Ariel Store and Tavern, near where Cooper jumped, holds a party to honour the "notorious antihero" and the hijacking's anniversary. One of the events is a D. B. lookalike contest.

The Lord Lucan Case

The sudden disappearance of Lord "Lucky" Lucan, accused of murdering his children's nanny in 1974, has captivated media outlets all over the world for decades. Every so often a story surfaces that the missing Earl has at last been found, but each time a solution to the mystery of his fate remains stubbornly, tantalizingly, out of reach.

———————————

"He really wanted to be rich.
To do the lovely things of life."

Jane Griffin, Lord Lucan's sister

———————————

At around 9:45 pm on 8 November 1974, a wide-eyed woman spattered with blood flung open the door of the Plumbers Arms pub at 14, Lower Belgrave Street, Belgravia, London. With one hand partly covering a large gash on her head, she screamed, "Help me, help me, I've just escaped being murdered! My children, my children, he's murdered my nanny!" The nanny was 29-year-old Sandra Rivett, and the terrified woman was Lady Veronica Lucan. Since that cold and misty night, police forces across the nation have been attempting to track down the alleged killer, her husband, Lord Lucan.

Richard John Bingham, 7th Earl of Lucan, commonly known as John, was born into an Anglo-Irish aristocratic family in Marylebone, a wealthy area in the West End of London, on 8 December 1934. John was the second child and oldest son of George Bingham, 6th Earl of Lucan, and Kaitlin Dawson. John's father was the descendant of George Bingham, 3rd Earl of Lucan, who gave the order for the Charge of the Light Brigade during the Crimean War. As World War II was approaching, John and his siblings, Jane, Sally, and Hugh, were sent to the safety of Toronto, Canada, and then Mount Kisco, New York. "It was a very quick decision that was made in England, and they had apparently 48 hours to decide, my parents, whether they would accept the berths that were available on the ship," said his elder sister, Jane.[1] They remained there for five years with the Brady Tuckers, one of the richest families in the United States.

The Brady Tuckers had made their wealth in finance at the end of the 19th century; they spent their winters on New York's Park Avenue, their summers on the beaches of Florida or on their estate at Mount Kisco.

According to Jane, when John was growing up, he was unusually restless and troubled, perhaps owing to his childhood upheavals. After his father inherited the earldom, John was sent to prestigious Eton College. "They thought that Eton would give him the extra attention needed – because he was showing signs, and I'm not sure what those signs were, of needing extra help. Not academically, but psychologically," said Jane. "I'm no psychiatrist but I think it well could have been to do with the separation from home at a young age, because I know for a fact that he was very, very unhappy." However, John seemingly thrived at Eton. It was here that he first acquired a taste for gambling and frequently bet on the dogs and horses at the nearby Windsor racecourse. "He really wanted to be rich. To do the lovely things of life," said Jane.

After leaving Eton in 1953, Lord John Bingham spent his two years of national service with the Coldstream Guards, the oldest regiment in the British army in continuous active service, in West Germany. His father, George, had been a distinguished Guards officer in World War II and had won the Military Cross. John Bingham spent most of his army career skiing on the slopes of the Swiss Alps or playing poker with fellow officers. Once back in London, Bingham seemingly settled easily into civilian life, joining the merchant bank William Brandt's Sons & Co. Over time, he became a skilful and experienced card player. After winning £26,000 at chemin de fer, a variety of baccarat, Bingham quit his lucrative position as a merchant banker to become a professional gambler. To his gambling buddies he was known as "Lucky Lucan" for his reckless gambling.

Lord Bingham became an early member of the exclusive Clermont Set, a group of high-stakes gamblers that met frequently at the Clermont Club, a London establishment that prided itself on its A-list membership. Founded in 1962 by gambler, businessman, and future zoo owner John Aspinall, the original crowd included five dukes, five marquesses, 20 earls, and two cabinet ministers. Among the movers and shakers who could be spotted at the club on any given night were author Ian Fleming, creator of James Bond; the Hollywood star Peter Sellers; and the artist Lucien Freud. Lucan became a popular figure in London society, known for his dashing good looks, prowess at gambling, and fondness for vodka martinis. He was even considered for the movie role of James Bond at one point.

In 1963, after a six-month courtship, Lord Bingham married Veronica Duncan, the daughter of an army major from a middle-class background. "I was looking for a god," she explained, "and he was a dream figure." The couple went on to have three children: Frances, born in 1964 – the year that Lord Bingham succeeded his father to the Lucan earldom – Camilla, born in 1970, and George, born in 1967. They settled into a lavish, Georgian-style home at 46, Lower Belgrave Street in the heart of London.

Although to his gambling friends Lord Lucan was known as "Lucky Lucan", his losses often exceeded his winnings. Gambling also took a toll on his marriage. Veronica suffered postpartum depression after the birth of each of her children, and the couple's marital difficulties were exacerbated when Lucan made her undergo psychiatric treatment. After running away from two psychiatric facilities, Veronica finally agreed to home visits and a course of anti-depressant drugs. Lucan subsequently began a campaign to brand Veronica mentally unstable, complaining to friends about her and claiming that she was violent.

Coinciding with his fast-disintegrating marriage, Lucan's wealth was hit by the combination of a stock market crash and big gambling losses. As his debts mounted, rifts in the marriage grew. Before long, Lord Lucan and Veronica were not only arguing about money, but also about how to raise their three children. By late 1972, Lucan had moved out of the family home to a bachelor apart-ment in Pimlico, just 0.4 km (a quarter of a mile) away.

In 1973, Lucan filed for custody of the children. In response, Veronica checked herself into the Priory Hospital in Roehampton, South West London, in order to prove that she was mentally fit and able to care for them herself. At the custody hearing, she testified that Lord Lucan was abusive and that he had tricked her into believing that she was mentally unstable in order to exert control over her – a tactic now known as gaslighting. The judge, Mr Justice Rees, sided with Veronica and concluded that Lord Lucan was an arrogant liar who lived an outrageous lifestyle that was unsuitable for bringing up children. In July 1973, Veronica was duly awarded full custody.

Lucan bitterly resented that the law considered Veronica a fit mother. Over the next year, hoping to win custody from her, he embarked on a spying campaign, secretly recording their phone calls in hopes that she would lose her temper and he could claim she was mentally unfit. He employed detectives to watch Veronica's every move and even made anonymous phone calls to her home.

November 7, 1974, was a gloomy, drizzly Thursday, typical of London in winter. That evening, Lord Lucan had planned a big dinner at the Clermont Club. The fact that he had successfully organized such an event was surprising because he owed the club £10,000 and his credit had been stopped by its new owners, the Playboy Club. They agreed to him holding the event there because it was good for business having such a respected and well-known figure frequenting their establishment. However, Lord Lucan never arrived for the scheduled dinner.

Around 9 pm, Veronica was watching television with her eldest child, Frances – George and Camilla were already in bed – at the family home at Lower Belgrave Street. Sandra Rivett, the children's nanny, usually took Thursdays off. However, on this particular Thursday she had asked Veronica whether she could work and take the following night off. It was Veronica's habit to make herself a cup of tea around this time. As she was working, Rivett offered to go downstairs to the basement kitchen to make the tea while Veronica watched television. Twenty minutes passed and Rivett did not return, so Veronica decided to investigate. Standing at the top of the stairs, she heard a noise. "I walked towards the sound," she recalled.[2] As she called out to Rivett, somebody lunged out of the shadows and cracked her over the head. When she began to scream, the assailant yelled, "Shut up!"

Veronica later told police, "I recognized the man by his voice. It was my husband!"[3]

Unknown to Veronica, whoever had just attacked her had, moments earlier, murdered Sandra Rivett. As Rivett entered the kitchen, she had been bludgeoned across the head several times with a lead pipe wrapped in tape. The attack was brutal and prolonged: Rivett's skull was split in six different places. Her body was then stuffed into a canvas mail sack, which was later found in the passage at the bottom of the stairs. Her pale hand was protruding out of the top and blood was seeping onto the parquet floor.

After Veronica was attacked from behind, her assailant stuck several fingers down her throat in an attempt to strangle her as she lay on the kitchen floor. In that life-or-death moment, Veronica managed to grab her attacker's testicles, causing him to release his grip. Veronica freed herself, got up off the floor, and turned – to see her husband standing before her. She told police that she asked him where Sandra Rivett was. At first, Lord Lucan claimed that she had gone out; then he confessed that he had "killed the nanny".[4]

According to Veronica, she and her husband sat together in the kitchen for a few moments, out of breath. They then both went upstairs. Lucan told Frances – who was still watching television – to go to bed, while Veronica went into the bathroom. "We went together into the bedroom . . . and together we looked at my injuries," Veronica said. "After we had done that, I think I said I don't feel very well, and he laid a towel on the bed, and I got on it." Veronica suggested to Lucan that he stay and take care of her for a few days. Once her injuries had healed, she would help him flee the country. They spoke for a few more minutes before Lucan went back into the bathroom to fetch a damp cloth to clean her face. "I heard the taps running and I jumped to my feet, out of the room, and down the stairs!" Veronica recalled.[5] She tore out of the front door and ran for help at the Plumbers Arms pub, some 27 m (30 yds) from the house.

Veronica was taken to St George's Hospital, Hyde Park, where she was treated for seven scalp wounds, cuts to the inside of her mouth, and shock. In time, she fully recovered from her physical injuries; however, the mental scars from her ordeal remained. Police issued a warrant for Lord Lucan's arrest, but he was nowhere to be found.

After fleeing the family home, Lucan telephoned his mother between 10:30 and 11 pm and detailed the "terrible catastrophe" that had occurred. He claimed that he had been driving past the house when he spotted, through the window, Veronica grappling with an intruder. Lucan said that he ran into the house and broke up the scuffle, allowing the alleged intruder to escape. He now feared that Veronica would accuse him of hiring the man to kill her. Lucan then drove to the country manor of a close friend, Ian Maxwell-Scott, in Uckfield, Sussex. Here, he wrote a somewhat cryptic, evasive letter to his wealthy brother-in-law, Bill Shand Kydd, that read:

> *"Dear Bill,*
>
> *The most ghastly circumstances arose this evening, which I briefly described to my mother. While I interrupted the fight* [Lucan refrained from explaining further] *at Lower Belgrave St and the man left Veronica accused me of having hired him. I took her upstairs and sent Frances up to bed and tried to clean her up. She lay doggo for a bit, and while I was in the bathroom left the house. The circumstantial evidence against me is strong in that V. will say that it was all my doing. I also will lie doggo for a bit but I am only concerned about the children. If you can manage it. I want them to live with you – Coutts (Trustees) St Martin's Lane (Mr Wall) will handle school fees. V. has demonstrated her hatred for me in the past and*

would do anything to see me accused. For George & Frances to go
through life knowing their father had stood in the dock for attempted
murder will be too much. When they are old enough to understand,
explain to them the dream of paranoia, and look after them.

Yours ever, John"⁶

After writing the letter, Lord Lucan left his friend's home and
drove off into the night.

In 1975, an inquest jury ruled that the person who killed Sandra
Rivett and attacked Veronica was Lord Lucan. Despite what he
had claimed in his letter to his brother-in-law, Veronica testified
that there was no man in the house other than him. Detectives
were also unable to find evidence of anybody else in the house.
They added that it would be extremely unlikely for someone
passing the house to be able to see a fight going on in the basement
through the venetian blinds. Lord Lucan was charged in absentia:
It was the first time in 200 years that a peer of the realm had been
accused of murder.

In the aftermath, Veronica was shunned by her friends. She
stunned the nation by saying that, despite the fact she believed the
assailant that attacked her had been her husband, she still loved
him. "My affections for him are as strong as they always have
been."

Lucan had left his affairs in a mess and Veronica was forced to
sell the family home and a number of personal belongings to pay
off his considerable debts. She once said that she believed that her
husband was still alive and that she was fully expecting him to
show up at her front door one day. She even said that she would
help pay for his defence. Veronica later changed her opinion of her

husband's fate, saying that she believed he had drowned himself in the English Channel.

The most widely accepted theory is that Lord Lucan had been planning to murder Veronica that night, but mistakenly attacked Sandra Rivett. Veronica and Rivett were about the same size and build, and Veronica often allowed Rivett to borrow her clothes. A basement lightbulb had been unscrewed and placed on a chair, so Lord Lucan would not have realized he was attacking the wrong woman. According to the police, the attack on his wife was Lord Lucan's final – and most desperate – gamble. Sandra Rivett's murder was simply a tragic case of mistaken identity.

Eventually the two detectives that originally headed the search for Lord Lucan, Superintendent Roy Ranson and Chief Inspector David Gerring, both retired from the force. Ranson believed that Lord Lucan was lying dead at the bottom of the English Channel. "If he were still alive, I feel sure we'd have had some hard information about him by now." Gerring, however, was sure that Lord Lucan had managed to flee the country. "I am convinced he is alive," he said. "Somebody is sending him money . . . A job would give him away."

The Lord Lucan case has become a staple of British criminal history, and theories as to what happened to him have abounded. To Lord Lucan's friends and family, he was set up by his spiteful wife. They pointed out that when Veronica burst through the doors of the Plumbers Arms exclaiming that "he" had attacked her, she never elaborated on who "he" was. Some speculated that, if Lord Lucan had committed murder, he would have taken his own life as "the honourable thing to do".[7] Others within his circle believed that Lord Lucan, being a professional gambler, would have assessed the odds and taken a chance on keeping his freedom, even at the cost of never seeing his children again. They also claimed that his actions after the attack were not consistent with someone planning to kill themselves

The day after the murder and attempted murder, Lord Lucan's abandoned car was discovered near Newhaven, East Sussex. In the boot, investigators found a length of lead pipe which appeared to be part of the same lead pipe found at the crime scene. They also found bloodstains – a mix of type A and type B. Significantly Veronica's blood group was type A; Sandra Rivett's was type B.

Police made an extensive search around the coast, cliffs, and caves in the Newhaven area, investigating the theory that Lord Lucan could have committed suicide. However, no body was discovered.

Detectives then focused on the theory that Lucan had fled abroad and assumed a new identity. At the time, there were two daily crossings between Newhaven and Dieppe, France. Police checked the country estates of all of Lord Lucan's French friends, yet none claimed to have seen him. The theory that Lord Lucan fled the country was certainly plausible. He had numerous wealthy friends in powerful and influential positions who would have been willing to assist him. In the aftermath of his disappearance, his aristocratic circle clammed up in a kind of conspiracy of silence that only deepened the mystery. Scotland Yard called in Interpol, and police in 119 countries were put on alert. The case was front-page news.

The most popular theory remains that Lord Lucan escaped the UK and lived a life of anonymity, and there have been numerous supposed sightings of him around the world, from Ireland and France to India, Africa, New Zealand, and Australia. One claimed that Lord Lucan was living in a Land Rover in New Zealand with a pet possum named Redfern and a goat named Camilla. Another asserted that Lord Lucan, now known as "Jungle Barry", was living a hippie lifestyle in India. In both cases, the men were ruled out as being Lord Lucan.[8]

In 1978, a burglary at Veronica's home set tongues wagging. The only things stolen were a photograph album and negatives of the couple's children. Had they been stolen, investigators wondered, to give solace to Lord Lucan in exile? The culprit was never caught.

One of the more lurid theories concerning Lord Lucan's fate was presented by Philippe Marcq, a friend of Lord Lucan and a regular at the Clermont Club. According to Marcq, following the murder, Lord Lucan travelled to Howletts Wild Animal Park in Kent, privately owned by Lucan's friend, John Aspinall (the park was not opened to the public until 1975). Lucan went there with a group of friends, and they discussed what Lord Lucan should do. According to Marcq: "They told him: 'Look, it is absolutely terrible what happened. You are a murderer. You tried to kill your wife out of desperation for your children and so they would be free from her influence. But what you have done makes absolutely sure she will be in control of your children for years to come. You are a murderer and you are going to be in a cell for the next 30 years.'" Lucan was advised that he needed to vanish without trace and, according to Marcq, he shot himself in the head in a room at the zoo. His body was then fed to a tiger named Zorra.[9]

According to the crime novelist Peter James, speaking at the Harrogate Crime Festival in July 2016, Lord Lucan escaped to Switzerland with the help of wealthy friends. James said that, once in Switzerland, Lord Lucan repeatedly attempted to contact his children and, fearful that his actions would lead the authorities to them, his friends decided to kill him. James alleged that he had been in contact with Lord Lucan's former circle, stating that, "One friend, most likely the late John Aspinall, told him, 'You're never going to see your kids again.' Aspinall and his friends panicked and thought they were done for. They had him bumped off in Switzerland, Mafia-style, and the body buried."

In the early 1980s, a witness on vacation in Africa told Detective Inspector Robert Polkinghorne, who was in charge of the case at the time, that he had seen Lord Lucan. However, despite the witness being thought credible, Scotland Yard refused funding for further investigations and the inquiry was discontinued.[10]

Richard Wilmott, author of *The Troops of Midian: Lucan's Flight to Freedom* in 2002, added weight to rumours that Lord Lucan had sought refuge in Africa. Wilmott, who had been researching the case for more than 20 years, claimed that Lucan's escape had been financed by several wealthy friends. Lucan was initially moved around the country from the Wellington Hotel in Tunbridge Wells, Kent, to the Crown Inn in the nearby village of Groombridge and from there to a safehouse in the Wiltshire Village of Fonthill Gifford. While hiding out there for a week, Lucan shaved off his moustache and bleached his hair. Then, using a phony passport provided to him by a former member of MI5, he boarded a flight to Athens from Heathrow airport. He travelled on to Crete and stayed at the remote Moni Kapsa monastery for several weeks before taking a boat to Africa. Wilmott claimed that his source for this information was James Gurney, a former MI5 agent. Gurney told Wilmott that he was a member of a right-wing "private army" known as the Troops of Midian – former government agents tasked to carry out "black ops" work for MI5, MI6, and even the CIA. "Everyone thought it was his wealthy chums that spirited him away, but it is just not possible to simply disappear without a trace.

Normal people, even those overburdened with wealth, lack the ability to pull off such a trick. It takes the hands of professionals to disappear completely for 40 years, and that's what he had," said Wilmott.[11]

Perhaps influenced by Wilmott's research, Superintendent Ranson, who worked on the original investigation, changed his stance on what became of Lord Lucan. He had previously believed that Lucan committed suicide. He now became a proponent of the theory that Lucan successfully escaped to Africa and started anew.[12]

In 2012, another player in the murder mystery finally broke her silence about the case after illness prompted her to review certain decisions she had made during her life. "Jill Findlay" (a pseudonym) was working as an assistant to John Aspinall at the time of the Rivett murder. She claimed that Aspinall instructed her to secretly send Lord Lucan's two oldest children to Africa, once in 1979 and then again in 1980. "It was in Gabon, from what I understand, that their father would observe them and see them, which is what he wanted to do," she recalled. "Just to see how they were growing up and look at them from a distance." Lucan's son, George, refuted this, stating that neither he nor his siblings had ever travelled to Africa.

In early 2020, Rivett's son, Neil Berriman, claimed that Lord Lucan was alive and living as a Buddhist in Australia. Berriman had spent tens of thousands of pounds in his quest to find out what had happened to Lord Lucan after the murder of his mother. His private investigations led him to the door of an ailing Englishman in an unnamed Australian city. This Englishman, whom Berriman believes is Lord Lucan, is said to be seriously ill and awaiting surgery. Berriman maintains that Lord Lucan was living in Africa until 2002, but then emigrated to Australia. Berriman presented his findings to Scotland Yard, who said that they will be investigating the tip.[13]

Lord Lucan was presumed dead in 1992; however, it was not until 3 February 2016 that his death certificate was issued, allowing his son to finally inherit the title 8th Earl of Lucan. In September the following year, 80-year-old Veronica was found dead in her London home. Police forced their way in after a friend reported not seeing her for several days. She was estranged from her sister, had five grandchildren that she had never met, and had lived alone for 40 years in a townhouse near where the crime had occurred. Cause of death was respiratory failure caused by barbiturates and alcohol poisoning. The coroner, Dr Fiona Wilcox, recorded a verdict of suicide.[14]

After her husband vanished, the lack of resolution in the case had haunted Veronica, pushing her to the brink of madness. She had lost custody of her children in 1982. On her website, lady-lucan.co.uk, she wrote that her son had declared that he would find it "much more congenial to live as part of the family of his aunt and uncle". Veronica did not attend the hearing nor did she apply for access. Veronica's sister, Christina Shand Kydd and her husband Bill, were subsequently granted custody of George, Frances, and Camilla. As they developed into adults, they called into question Veronica's version of events.

Veronica spent her final years as a recluse. "I tried to commit suicide but it didn't work. I've been celibate since the age of 35 and now I have no friends," she said in a 1998 interview with the *Independent* newspaper. "Society has shunned me for my husband's crime. I don't care what happens anymore. I'm waiting to die – a nice heart attack would suit me fine."[15] She left her £576,626 estate to the homelessness charity Shelter.[16]

The "Case of the Vanishing Earl", as it is sometimes known, shocked the British aristocracy to its foundations. For years, hardly a day went by without the name Lord Lucan appearing in British newspapers. With its glamorous aura of aristocratic excess, a dysfunctional marriage, a murder, and a disappearance, the saga captivated – and continues to captivate – the public imagination.

The Rendlesham Forest Incident

In late December 1980, a group of American airmen from a US Air Force base at Woodbridge, Suffolk, saw strange lights in the sky. A short while later, they claimed to have encountered a UFO in nearby Rendlesham Forest. What they saw that night would become one of the UK's most famous UFO sightings, one that has fully justified the moniker "Britain's Roswell".

———————

"I can tell you this, we are not alone."

Former US Air Force Lt Col. Charles I. Halt

———————

In 1980, Royal Air Force Woodbridge and Royal Air Force Bentwaters were part of a US Air Force complex that was nestled among the dense, predominantly coniferous woodland of Rendlesham Forest, near the Suffolk coast. They were frontline defenders of Britain's security. At the height of the Cold War with the Soviet Union there were at least 13,000 US servicemen stationed at the two bases, as well as a number of nuclear weapons.[1]

At around 3 am on 26 December 1980, two USAF security police patrolmen from RAF Woodbridge noticed unusual lights around 1.6 km (1 mile) from the back gate. Initially, Sgt Jim Penniston and Airman First Class John Burroughs thought that an aircraft must have crashed in Rendlesham Forest. They asked for permission to leave the base and investigate. The on-duty flight chief told them to search the area on foot, taking along Airman First Class Ed Cabansag. His role was to stay in their truck and maintain radio contact with Penniston and Burroughs.

What the two men saw next was reported by deputy base commander Lieutenant Colonel Charles I. Halt in a USAF memo. After walking between 1.6 and 3.2 km (1 and 2 miles) – accounts vary – into the forest, Penniston and Burroughs claimed they encountered a glowing object. It was metallic, triangular in shape, and around 2.7 m (9 ft) wide by 1.8 m (6 ft) high. The object "illuminated the entire forest with a white light and had a pulsing red light on top and a bank of blue lights underneath", reported Halt.[2] It was either hovering or standing on short legs, and as the men drew closer, they began experiencing interference on their radios. In 2010, Penniston recalled, "At first, I was confused, not understanding what I was seeing. This was truly unbelievable. Then fear struck me, but I told myself I had to stay focused. Was this a threat to the base and to us? I had to determine that first and foremost."[3] As the patrolmen approached the strange object, it moved away from them, as if under intelligent control, slowly passing through the trees and onto nearby farmland, where it caused some disturbance among livestock. Penniston and Burroughs climbed a fence that separated the forest trees from an open field. "You could see the lights down by a farmer's field," recollected Burroughs. They started walking towards the light. Then, in an instant, it vanished.

Penniston later claimed that, while in the forest that night, he had seen hieroglyphic-like characters on the side of the UFO – a triangle surrounded by other symbols. He claimed he drew the patterns he saw in a notebook. "They were etched into the surface of the craft," said Penniston. "I put my hand on the craft and it was warm to the touch. The surface was smooth, like glass, but it had the quality of metal, and I felt a constant low voltage running through my hand and moving to my mid-forearm." Burroughs had no recollection of any of this. Subsequently, commentators speculated that the symbols could have been binary code, and Penniston would claim in 2010, while under hypnosis, that a binary code was downloaded directly into his brain when he touched the UFO.

Penniston and Burroughs radioed RAF Woodbridge's security

desk to report what they had seen and the base contacted Suffolk police to report "a sighting of some unusual lights in the sky". Two police officers investigated and reported back: "Air Traffic Control checked. No knowledge of aircraft. Reports received of aerial phenomena over southern England during the night. Only lights visible in this area was from Orford Ness Lighthouse [some 9.7 km (6 miles) away]. Search made of area – negative."[4] The following day, however, police returned to the scene at the request of the Bentwaters base's security officer, Wing Commander Gordon Williams, who claimed that they had "found a place where a craft of some sort seems to have landed, two miles east of the East Gate".[5] According to Williams, they had found three shallow depressions in the ground where Penniston and Burroughs had claimed to see the UFO. These depressions were 3.8 cm (1½ in) deep and 17.8 cm (7 in) wide. There were also burn marks on nearby trees and broken branches in the surrounding area.[6] PC Brian Cresswell attended the scene, but was unimpressed. "There were three marks in the area which did not follow a set pattern. The impressions made by these marks were of no depth and could have been made by an animal."

On 27 December, the twin bases' annual Christmas party was interrupted by Lt Bruce Englund. He told Lt Col. Halt that strange lights had been seen and that "It" was back. Halt headed out to Rendlesham Forest with several servicemen, expecting to be able to debunk this supposed UFO sighting. His men were equipped with Geiger counters and took radiation readings of three depressions that they discovered in the ground. The readings showed high levels of radiation, around seven or eight times what would have been expected for that area.

Meanwhile, a USAF Sergeant stationed at RAF Bentwaters,

Adrian Bustinza, had caught wind of what was unfolding at Rend-lesham Forest. He assembled a number of military personnel and they set off for the scene.

At around 11 pm, Bustinza's group came across Halt and his men. Larry Warren – an 18-year-old soldier serving with the US Air Force security police with Bustinza, recalled, "We were all told to hand in our weapons. I had an M16 rifle."[1] As Halt and his men continued their investigation, they noticed strange sounds coming from nearby farm animals. Moments later, a red sun-like light was spotted moving and pulsing through the trees. "I see it too . . . it's back again . . . it's coming this way . . . there's no doubt about it . . . this is weird . . . it looks like an eye winking at you . . . it almost burns your eyes . . . he's coming toward us now . . . now we're observing what appears to be a beam coming down to the ground . . . one object is still hovering over Woodbridge base . . . beaming down,"[7] said Halt into his voice recorder.

According to Warren, however, the incident was even more bizarre than Halt's voice recording. In fact, years later, Warren's account would become a topic of particular controversy. He described the object as "the size of a basketball, an American basket-ball", that was "self-illuminated, not quite red".[8] He claimed that this bright object suddenly exploded and a craft appeared on the forest ground right before them. He described this craft as having "no windows, no markings, no flag or country of origin. Nothing. You could hardly look at it head on, and if you looked at it through the side of your peripheral vision, you'd get the shape of it . . . and there it was, clear as a bell". Warren claims that he and Bustinza were asked to leave the area by a senior officer. From a distance, he claimed that he saw Wing Commander Gordon Williams approach the craft and then have some kind of encounter with an alien, which

Warren described as a "silent standoff". Williams himself has never gone on record or publicly spoken about the Rendlesham Forest Incident.

In Halt's version of events, however, nobody was close enough to the strange object to approach it. Instead, he described the object zigzagging through the trees as they moved closer to try and inspect it. Suddenly, it took off without any noise and at an unbelievable speed. It appeared to leave a trail of particles behind it before breaking into five separate white objects and disappearing. Halt described the object in the forest as like "nothing I have ever seen before" and also described a yellow mist drifting through the trees. According to Halt's memo, moments after observing the UFO take off, three star-like objects were noticed in the sky, two to the north and one to the south. All of these objects were said to be 10 degrees off the horizon. They moved rapidly in sharp angular movements and displayed red, green, and blue lights. When the objects in the north were looked at through an 8-12–power lens, they could not be identified. Moments later, they appeared to lose their star-like shape and instead transformed into circles. The objects in the north remained in the sky for over an hour, while the object in the south was visible for two to three hours. From time to time, it beamed down a stream of light. Halt later commented, "Here I am, a senior official who routinely denies this sort of thing and diligently works to debunk them [i.e. UFOs], and I'm involved in the middle of something I can't explain." Bustinza's version of events agreed with Halt's account.

It was not until 1983, after Halt's memo was released under the United States Freedom of Information Act, that the Rendlesham Forest Incident gained national publicity. "If the memo had not been released, I would have continued to remain silent," said Halt.

"This experience is not something I ever wanted to speak about publicly."

Since then, what truly occurred that night has become increasingly hazy. Hard evidence of the Rendlesham Forest Incident is lacking, statements have changed, and new witnesses have come forward. As is the case with the majority of UFO sightings, rumours soon spread of some kind of military cover-up. The official response, as encapsulated in a Ministry of Defence statement released in 2002 under the UK's Freedom of Information Act, was certainly clear: "No evidence was found of any threat to the defence of the United Kingdom, and no further investigations were carried out. No further information has come to light which alters our view that the sightings of these lights was of no defence significance."

The cause of the mystery has been variously explained as a military training exercise, an elaborate hoax, a UFO encounter, a meteor shower, a rogue satellite, and the beam from Orford Ness Lighthouse.

Ian Ridpath, editor of *The Oxford Dictionary of Astronomy,* is a staunch backer of the lighthouse-beam theory. After reviewing a transcript of a live tape recording made by Lt Col. Halt while investigating the UFO with his men, Ridpath came to the conclusion that Halt had mistaken the stars Vega, Deneb, and Sirius, as well as beams from the Orford Ness Lighthouse and possibly the Shipwash Lightship, for UFO activity.

The lighthouse theory, however, does have its drawbacks. The strange lights were first noticed by USAF security police patrolmen Penniston and Burroughs from the back gate of RAF Woodbridge; however, the beacon of the Orford Ness Lighthouse cannot be seen from this location. Furthermore, every resident in the area knew about the lighthouse and it seems unlikely that it would have confused so many witnesses. "Lighthouses don't fly," Halt once quipped.[9] In 2010, Halt confirmed that while in Rendlesham Forest that night, he and his men saw the beam from the Orford Ness Lighthouse and the mysterious lights at the same time.

Ridpath also put forward the theory that what was seen that night in the sky was a fireball, explaining, "Brilliant fireballs like this, caused by natural pieces of debris from space burning up in the atmosphere, are a major cause of UFO reports." At 2:50 am on 26 February 1980, four witnesses in southern England (the exact location was not reported) reported seeing "a fireball" in the sky. "[A] fireball is most likely what they saw, and . . . nothing landed in Rendlesham Forest," commented Ridpath.[10]

Another proposed explanation was that the UFO was some kind of secret prototype aircraft or even a drone. It has also been suggested that the strange symbols that Penniston claimed he saw may have been Cyrillic script, indicating that the UFO was a Soviet craft. Building on this premise, some commentators have considered that the UFO and lights were some kind of military psychological operation, and that the witnesses were nothing more than human test subjects, manipulated to see how they would react to an unusual experience. It was also suggested that this military psychological operation had involved seemingly solid objects generated by holographic technology.

Another theory with an added Soviet Union twist was put forward in 1998 by Ufologist Jenny Randles, author of *UFO: Crash Landing? Friend or Foe?* Shortly after 9 pm on 25 December 1980, the USSR's Cosmos 749 rocket re-entered Earth's atmosphere over northwestern Europe. Randles suggested that the National Security Agency (NSA) at Orford Ness had fired an energy beam "to jam the electronics on the Soviet military satellite and deflect its orbital path, causing it to burn up in a controlled fashion". While it was thought that the Cosmos 749 rocket had broken up during re-entry and burned out somewhere east of Clacton, in the neighbouring county of Essex, Randles suggested in her follow-up book, *The UFOs That Never Were*, that the flightpath of the incoming debris was altered "as if something caused the trajectory to be deflected".[11]

Since going public, Halt has said that many other witnesses have come to him privately to reveal that they witnessed something strange in the sky that night. He said that two air-traffic control tower operators at RAF Bentwaters saw an object that they could not identify and also observed something cross their screen. According to Halt, other witnesses came forward with similar accounts, but they had been ordered by somebody "up the chain of command" to stay silent about what they had seen. The two air-traffic controllers, Ike Barker and Jim Carey, went public in 2016 in the television documentary *UFOs and Nukes: The Secret Link Revealed*. According to Barker: "It was travelling at an extremely high rate of speed. It passed over the control tower and then it stopped." Jim Carey agreed, stating that, "It was just phenomenal to see it go that fast. I said, 'That can't be one of ours.'"[12]

In 2010, Halt stated in a signed affidavit, "I believe the objects I saw at close quarters were extraterrestrial in origin and that the security services of both the United States and the United Kingdom have attempted – both then and now – to subvert the significance of what occurred at Rendlesham Forest and RAF Bentwaters by the use of well-practised methods of disinformation."[13] He also stated that he was tired "of all the disinformation out there. It seems that every time I turn around, I hear more nonsense or am accused of something". He confessed that before that night, he was a UFO sceptic and that he "never really gave [UFOs] a second thought before the incident".[14]

Halt has maintained that agents from the US's Office of Special Investigations had secretly investigated the incident in the days that followed. He alleged that witnesses were told by agents not to speak about what they had seen that night or they would lose their jobs. "Drugs such as sodium pentothal, often called a truth serum, when used with some form of brainwashing or hypnosis, were administered during these interrogations, and the whole thing has had damaging, and lasting, effects on the men involved," said Halt. In 2015, John Burroughs won compensation for illnesses that he blamed on exposure to radiation from the Rendlesham Forest Incident.

Another person who maintained that there was definitely an extraterrestrial presence in the forest that night was the pseudonymous "Steve Roberts", an airman at the base at the time. According to Roberts, he was one of the group on patrol with Sgt Bustinza. In 1981, he claimed, like Larry Warren, that he had witnessed Wing Commander Gordon Williams approaching the UFO. He alleged that everybody else present was ordered back while Williams had some kind of communication with the aliens that were beside the UFO. According to Roberts, it looked as though Williams was using some kind of sign language to communicate with them. He described the aliens as about 0.9 m (3 ft) tall and wearing "all-over" silver suits. He said that they appeared to hover close to the ground and were suspended in a shaft of light that projected from the underside of the UFO.

Roberts' account – much like Warren's – has been met with widespread scepticism owing to lack of corroboration. While both men claimed that there was a number of other servicemen present, they are the only two to claim they saw extraterrestrials. In an interview with the *News of the World* newspaper on 28 September 1983, Warren changed his story and claimed that he didn't actually see any aliens himself, stating, "I realized the spaceship was inhabited. There were beings aboard. I didn't see them because I was on the wrong side of the craft. But others did. They said there were three, and they were wearing silver suits." In the same interview, he claimed that he "had a strange feeling and seemed to black out", adding that "the next thing I knew, it was about 5 am and I was waking up lying half across my bunk. I still had my uniform on and was up to my knees in mud. To this day, I don't know how I got back to the barracks".

Halt has utterly dismissed claims that aliens – or images of aliens – were present at the scene, describing them as "pure fiction".[1]

In 1998, Warren published a book on his supposed experiences in Rendlesham Forest titled *Left at East Gate: A First-Hand Account of the Bentwaters-Woodbridge Incident, Its Cover-up, and Investigation*, which he co-authored with the investigative writer and UFO specialist Peter Robbins. However, in 2017, their relationship deteriorated when Robbins accused Warren of "deceiving him" with a false account of what took place that night. Speaking in May of that year to the Inception Radio Network, a show specializing in the paranormal, Robbins said, "Over the past year, even a bit more, highly specific information has been brought to my attention that has disturbed me tremendously." He expressed that he had wholeheartedly believed in Warren's version of events and that was why he had agreed to co-author the book. "I felt I had proved enough to myself of Larry's account and details surrounding it that he was telling the truth. And I feel now that in part that was not the case and there was an intent to deceive. To say this has tore me up over the last year is an understatement." Following this revelation, the American publisher,

Cosimo, announced that it would be suspending the distribution of Warren and Robbins' book, stating, "Recently, it has been brought to our attention that some of the experiences described in this book may be inaccurate or embellished."

By this point, other witnesses and commentators had also questioned Warren's credibility. Bustinza had publicly stated that he couldn't remember Warren even being in Rendlesham Forest that night and suggested that Warren had taken information about what he, Bustinza, had seen in the forest and reworked it to create his own story.

Finally, it is possible that the entire Rendlesham Forest Incident was an elaborate prank. In 2016, Dr David Clark, a lecturer at Sheffield Hallam University, received an anonymous tip from a man who claimed to have been a member of the Special Air Service (SAS) at the time. Dr Clark's informant asserted that the entire Rendlesham Forest Incident was a hoax perpetrated by the British SAS on the American personnel stationed at Bentwaters and Woodbridge bases. Dr Clark spent three years looking into this claim and came to believe that it was credible. Apparently, the SAS used to regularly test US security by probing the perimeters of the twin air force bases in Rendlesham Forest. Dr Clark suggested that in August 1980, SAS soldiers had parachuted into Woodbridge Air Force Base to test its defences and, to their considerable embarrassment, had been caught, imprisoned for 18 hours, and subjected to extensive interrogation by US personnel, who didn't believe they were SAS soldiers at all. Their interrogators kept referring to them as "aliens". Dr Clark claimed that the word "aliens" stuck in the minds of these SAS troopers and they decided to hatch a revenge plan, by rigging up lights and coloured flares in the forest using black helium balloons and remote-controlled kites.

Dr Clark's hoax theory, like all the others, has met with criticism. Nick Pope, a Ministry of Defence employee from 1985 to 2006, conducted a cold-case review of the incident during his tenure and co-authored the landmark book, *You Can't Tell the People* with UFO researcher Georgina Bruni. According to Pope, "I'm sceptical of this latest theory . . . [and] I can confirm that no explanation for the Rendlesham Forest Incident was ever found. We looked at all the theories – and the claim that this was a prank isn't new – and none of them fits the facts."[15]

During his time at the Ministry of Defence, Pope was tasked with evaluating UFO sightings and determining whether any of them posed a threat to the defence of the United Kingdom. Each case was thoroughly investigated and Pope determined that between 90 and 95 percent of UFO sightings could be attributed to the misidentification of ordinary objects or phenomena. However, there remained a small handful that "defied conventional explanation and involved what appeared to be a structured craft of unknown origin, capable of manoeuvres and speeds beyond the abilities of anything in our inventory – prototype craft included."

Pope's investigations appeared to point to some kind of official cover-up, or at least to official negligence. In the Ministry of Defence's Rendlesham Forest case file, there was evidence that General Gabriel, Commander in Chief of the US Air Force in Europe, had visited the Woodbridge base following the incident and taken possession of Lt Col. Halt's tape recordings. Pope also found that the original inquiries by the USAF had been "fundamentally flawed by procedural errors, delay, and poor information sharing. The USAF had not cordoned off the landing site, taken soil samples, or used metal detectors to search the area". Pope also stated that the USAF did not pass on a number of witness statements, including a sketch that Penniston had made of the UFO. Critically, the USAF had conducted no follow-up interviews with key witnesses, including Lt Col. Halt.

Pope believed that these failings resulted from confusion about jurisdiction; each party thought that the other should have been investigating the incident. When the senior USAF officer in the UK, General Robert Bazley, was briefed on the incident by Wing Commander Williams, the officer in command of RAF Woodbridge and RAF Bentwaters at the time, he was told that the incident was "a Brit affair" because it had taken place off base. Pope said that both the Ministry of Defence and the USAF had been ordered to "play down" the UFO element and the extent of official involvement. Therefore, confusion over jurisdiction suited both parties, who could each claim that the other was investigating the incident.

The Rendlesham Forest Incident remains Britain's most tantalizing alleged "encounter of the third kind". Sadly, over time, the case has been engulfed by misinformation, disinformation, confabulation, and secrecy. Many new witnesses have come forward, while many original witnesses have changed their accounts, only deepening the mystery of the case. Nevertheless, the enthusiasm of Ufologists has never wavered and has even intensified over time. The incident has inspired numerous books, each one of which puts forward another theory as to what happened in Rendlesham Forest that night. In fact, Forestry England has capitalized on the affair by creating a UFO trail that meanders through the dense woodland.

"I can tell you this, we are not alone," said Halt in an interview with local newspaper the *Ipswich Star,* 6 September 2018. "I'm not telling you there's somebody walking around here that's an alien. There's some type of presence here . . ."[16]

Skinwalker Ranch

In the late 1990s and early 2000s, the land surrounding Skinwalker Ranch, Utah, became the scene of a barrage of paranormal and unexplainable phenomena. These included UFO encounters, strange balls of light, animal mutilations, and monstrous, seemingly invulnerable creatures.

"It's as if some cosmic puppet master had written a laundry list of every spooky phenomenon of modern times."

Investigative journalist George Knapp

In the summer of 1996, Colm Kelleher, a research immunologist at the National Jewish Medical and Research Center in Denver, came across an intriguing job advertisement in a scientific magazine. It was asking for scientists interested in "exploring the origin and evolution of consciousness in the universe." Kelleher decided to respond because he had a long-standing interest in scientific anomalies. He soon joined a team of research scientists with backgrounds in physics, biochemistry, and veterinary studies working for the National Institute of Discovery Science (NIDS).

NIDS had been founded by Las Vegas real-estate and aerospace tycoon Robert Bigelow, who wanted to remove the "crackpot element" from the study of anomalous phenomena. Bigelow's grandparents believed that they had once seen a UFO in 1947 while driving across the Nevada desert, and from childhood on he had been fascinated with the paranormal, the mysterious, and the unexplained.[1] By founding NIDS, Bigelow hoped to assemble a team of scientists who would study paranormal phenomena from an unbiased, scientific angle.

Kelleher and the other scientists soon found themselves at 194-hectare (480-acre) Skinwalker Ranch, bordering the Ute Indian

Reservation in west Uintah County, Utah. Bigelow had purchased it in 1996 for $200,000 after a series of unaccountable occurrences had terrorized its preceding owners, the Sherman family.

The Shermans — Terry, Gwen, and their two children (whose names were never publicly revealed) — had moved to isolated Skinwalker Ranch in 1994 to raise cattle. Terry had advanced training in animal husbandry and had plans to raise hybrid animals. The ranch had sat idle for seven years after its previous owners virtually abandoned it, returning only a couple of times a year to make sure that the fence lines were still intact.[2] Skinwalker was located about 5 km (3 miles) down a dirt trail from the nearest main road. The family, who were looking for peace and privacy, thought it was perfect, and were surprised that the preceding family had attached bolts to the ranch house's doors and windows, and even to kitchen cabinets. On both sides of the house, iron stakes were embedded in the ground with heavy chains attached to them.[3] Terry Sherman assumed that the previous owners must have kept large guard dogs, but he wasn't sure why. The whole area was safe, quiet, and virtually crime-free. The ranch was in need of extensive renovations, which the Shermans enthusiastically undertook, determined to create their dream home.

Their tranquillity would soon be interrupted, however, by a series of inexplicable, often disturbing events.

Shortly after they moved in, Terry left the ranch to check on a cow that was calving in the pasture to the south of the ranch when he noticed a peculiar light in a field. The light could not have been caused by neighbours or passing cars — the main road was too far away. "It went over some poplar trees there that are probably 40 to 50 feet [12 to 15 m] tall," said Terry to the *Deseret News* in 1996.[4]

This was the first UFO sighting on the ranch, but it certainly wouldn't be the last. During their time at Skinwalker, Terry, Gwen, and their children witnessed myriad different UFOs and mysterious lights. They described a small, box-like craft with a white light, a 12-m (40-ft) craft, and an extremely large craft that they estimated to be the size of several football fields. They also described watching a number of strange lights appear in the sky, including orange circular ones that appeared in mid-air. These lights appeared quite frequently, and sometimes the Shermans would see objects seemingly flying out of these orange lights, as if they were windows into another dimension.

One night, one of these lights seemingly followed Gwen's car home. On another night, Terry witnessed a light that appeared to be hiding behind a rock ridge, as if it were trying to avoid him as he walked towards it. Terry concealed himself behind a hay bale. Moments later, the light appeared again. This time, however, it looked as though it was flying back and forth, almost as if it were looking for Terry. Terry decided he would try to "sneak up on the object". As it came closer, he jumped out from behind the hay bale and began shouting and waving his hands. The light flashed on and off three times before disappearing.

Terry and Gwen noted that the lights mostly occurred during a new moon or when the sky was overcast or stormy.

Meanwhile, mysterious events were happening thick and fast on Skinwalker Ranch. One afternoon, the Shermans came across three strange circles arranged about 9 m (30 ft) apart in the shape of a triangle. Nearby, they found further circles in the soil. They were about 90 cm (3 ft) wide and 30 cm (1 ft) deep, and the soil in the centre of each circle was perfectly flat. On another occasion, the family heard noises of machinery that seemed to be coming from under the ground.

Quite often, the Shermans would lose items, only to have them turn up in odd places on the ranch. On several occasions, Gwen emerged from the shower to discover that her towel and personal items were missing from the locked bathroom. On another occasion, Terry lost a post digger, only to find it later, perched high up in a tree. One afternoon, Gwen arrived home with some groceries; she put them away, but when she went back into the kitchen, the groceries were back out on the kitchen table.

Instances of unexplained phenomena went further than lights and unseen forces. The Shermans also witnessed physical manifestations that could not be explained. They reported seeing huge wolf-like creatures on the ranch, as well as dark, bipedal creatures that stood around 2.7 m (9 ft) tall, comparable to the legendary, ape-like Sasquatch or Bigfoot.[5] One of the creatures that resembled an abnormally large wolf attacked a cow in broad daylight. Terry shot it several times, but his bullets seemingly had no effect and there was no blood. When the animal finally ran off towards some trees, Terry followed its footprints until they inexplicably disappeared.

The Shermans also described seeing a creature with curly red hair walking on all fours, which then attacked one of their horses. According to Terry, the beast was "low to the ground, heavily muscled, weighing perhaps 200 pounds [90 kg], with curly red hair and a bushy tail." When Terry approached the animal, it vanished. Another frightening creature the Shermans saw was almost transparent. It moved at great speed and let out a deep roar, like a cross between a bear and a lion. Later, they said this animal was comparable to the alien lifeform in the movie *Predator*.

One afternoon when Terry was out on the range, he heard male voices speaking an unfamiliar language. Terry was adamant that the disembodied voices were coming from around 7.6 m (25 ft) above him; however, he couldn't see a thing. As he stood perplexed, trying to ascertain what exactly he was hearing and where it was coming from, his dogs became frantic, barking and growling at something before running back to the ranch. On another occasion, Terry discovered four of his prize bulls stuffed inside a trailer with the door secured shut. "For a long time, we wondered what we were seeing, if it was something to do with a top-secret project," said Terry. "I don't know really what to think about it . . ."[1]

To add to this already bizarre catalogue of events, the Sherman family reported that their cattle began turning up dead. One cow had a hole, around 15 cm (6 in) wide by 2.5cm (1 in) deep, carved out of its rectum. Another one was found with a missing eyeball. In addition to the two mutilated cows, four completely vanished without a trace. In one instance, Terry noticed that there were hoofprints leading to a field that abruptly stopped near some trees. Around the final cluster of hoofprints, Terry noticed a circle of broken twigs and branches. Furthermore, the treetops appeared to have been cut off. Terry wondered whether something had come down from the sky and abducted the cow. "It was just gone. It was very bizarre."

Terry said that several other ranchers had called the police to report mutilation of their livestock, but they had been told that there was nothing the police could do about it. However, Sheriff Ralph Stansfield of Duchesne County claimed that he was unaware of any reports of UFO sightings or livestock mutilations within the time frame. Terry was distinctly unimpressed. "We've seen the UFOs enough and we know pretty much what the craft look like, and I think it's definitely associated with the cattle mutilations – when we see the crafts and then the cattle, we have problems," Terry said.

In fact, at various times in the past, several local people had witnessed things that they could not explain. Leland Mecham, who lived in Neola, Duchesne County, allegedly witnessed UFOs twice – once in the mid-1960s and another in the mid-1970s. He described the second craft as a massive object with colourful rays of light emanating from underneath. He said it appeared to be scanning the area before ascending, shooting across the sky, and vanishing. "There's no way it was swamp gas or balloons like everybody tries to pass it off," he said.

Retired high-school science teacher Joseph Hicks spent years researching the area's paranormal sightings after another teacher witnessed a UFO with his students back in 1951. "It was cigar-shaped, sitting on the ground during daylight, and was seen by 30 students and their teacher from about 50 feet [15 m] away . . ." He estimated that at least half of the 50,000 residents of the Uintah basin had seen unexplained objects in the sky, and he himself claimed to have witnessed a UFO over the city of Roosevelt, Utah, in the mid-1970s.[6]

Hicks' research led him to investigate the history of the area. Skinwalker Ranch is surrounded by the Uintah and Ouray Indian Reservation, and members of the Ute people lived in the region for centuries, long before European settlers arrived in the mid-1800s. The Ute fought to expel the Navajo from the area shortly before the settlers arrived. The Navajo eventually left the area to the Ute, but, according to legend, they left upon them the curse of the "skinwalker", a witch that could take on the form of a human or an animal that could not be killed. "The Navajos lost and then, in turn, cursed the Utes with the skinwalker, saying a spiritual person that changes into a wolf will be here to harass you, and they accepted that," explained Hicks. "It all seems to be concentrated on the ranch. The Utes don't mess with it. They have stories about the place that go back 15 generations. They say the ranch is in the path of the skinwalker."[2]

One of the most distressing encounters for the Shermans took place in May 1996. As night was falling, a blue orb appeared in the sky, darting around a field near the ranch. The Shermans had seen these blue orbs numerous times by now. While these lights seemed innocuous, the sight of them always left the family feeling anxious and fearful. On this occasion, Terry encouraged three of his dogs to pursue the orb. The dogs chased the light into the trees bordering the ranch. They disappeared out of sight, but moments later Terry heard the sound of distressed yelps, followed by complete silence. The three dogs never returned, no matter how much Terry called them. The following morning, Terry set out to look for them. Just past the treeline, he found three spots with a black greasy lump in the middle of each one. Terry was sure that the dogs had been incinerated by something.[7]

In the summer of 1996, the *Deseret News* ran an article about the Sherman family and the strange occurrences at their ranch. Terry hadn't wanted to go public, but, by this point, the family was desperate for answers. After reading the article, Robert Bigelow flew out to Utah and made the Sherman family an offer they couldn't refuse: $200,000 for the ranch. The Sherman family moved to a smaller homestead around 24 km (15 miles) away, but stayed on as ranchers and caretakers at Skinwalker Ranch. They had to sign non-disclosure agreements forbidding them from speaking about scientific activity on the ranch.

"At the end, the family was sleeping on the floor in one room together," commented investigative journalist George Knapp, the co-author, with Colm A. Kelleher, of *Hunt for the Skinwalker* in

2005. In the years that followed, many would question why the family stayed on at the ranch for so long – almost two years. According to Kelleher, Terry was a proud and stubborn man who, for quite a while, had concluded that the military was behind the unexplained phenomena and had turned his ranch into a testing ground for advanced military equipment. He didn't want to leave because "he was going to catch them".[8] By the time Terry went to *Deseret News*, however, he had abandoned this conclusion and was convinced that the events were supernatural in origin.

Bigelow moved his NIDS team to Skinwalker and they set up an observation post and equipped the ranch with video cameras and audio recording equipment, observing it 24 hours a day. "Our approach is to do good, high-quality research using a standard scientific approach and do what we can to get hard data," said John B. Alexander, member of NIDS and former director of non-lethal weapons testing at Los Alamos National Laboratories in New Mexico.[9]

The phenomena that had plagued the Sherman family continued. Over the next few months, the scientists allegedly saw large, ferocious animals with piercing yellow or red eyes. Although seen, these creatures left no visible tracks, and when the scientists attempted to shoot them, they were seemingly invulnerable. One evening, two of the scientists and Terry spotted a large animal in the branches of a tree with another large animal at the base of the tree. The animal in the branches was described as having "reptilian eyes" and a head that was around 0.9 m (3 ft) wide. The one at the base of the tree was described as a massive, dog-like creature. Terry aimed his hunting rifle at the animals. The one at the bottom of the tree vanished before he could fire, while the one in the branches fell out of the tree. However, when Terry and the others searched for its body, it was nowhere to be seen.

On one occasion in winter, the scientists came across a perfectly round ice circle on the ground, much like a crop circle. No footprints surrounded the ice circle, and the ice was too thin to support much weight. The scientists also reported that they witnessed what they could only describe as a rectangular portal that opened in the ground. On several occasions, the NIDS team saw orbs and UFOs in the sky, yet when they meticulously placed audio and video recording devices around the ranch to catch evidence of anything anomalous, they recorded nothing. However, they did notice a pattern. If the scientists placed extra cameras and personnel in the southern field, the mysterious activity would intensify in the northern field and vice versa.

In another inexplicable incident, equipment set up by the scientists was vandalized and wiring was shredded. This equipment was in direct view of a remote camera, but when the NIDS team reviewed the footage, expecting to discover who – or what – had caused the damage, they saw nothing. "It was very difficult to gather the kind of evidence consistent with scientific publication," observed Kelleher.[10] In addition, most of the paranormal events on Skinwalker Ranch only happened a few times, making them impossible to study in sufficient detail.

One of the most disturbing events took place at around 10 am on 10 March 1997. Terry and Gwen were out in the pasture tagging calves; they tagged one and weighed it at 38 kg (84 lb). Other than a strange, musky odour, everything seemed to be normal. They left the calf with its mother and continued with their duties. Around 40 minutes later, the Shermans' dog began growling and raising his hackles. The Shermans had not noticed anything out of the ordinary or heard any strange noises. The dog then took off. It was never seen again. The Shermans walked back through the pasture and spotted the mother of the calf they had tagged earlier running around in a half-circle, limping. As they approached the mother, they spotted the calf. It was torn open and spreadeagled on the ground. Vital organs were missing, as well as one of its ears. Nearby, they found one of the calf's femurs picked clean. However, there was not a trace of blood on the ground or on the calf. In just 40 minutes, some unseen force had entered the field and carefully torn the calf apart without anybody seeing or hearing a thing.

The Shermans called NIDS, who had taken a rare weekend off and returned to Las Vegas, to report their grim discovery. When the scientific team arrived at the scene, a veterinarian noticed that the missing ear appeared to have been surgically removed. A sniffer dog was unable to pick up the scent of any other animal, and NIDS was unable to find any tracks of a vehicle or footprints. "The bottom line is this animal must have been killed elsewhere because there was no blood at the scene, and then the animal must have been brought back, laid down carefully, almost ritually on the spot where it had been tagged," said Kelleher. NIDS were unable to determine what had caused the mutilation but said that it must have been mechanical. It was evident that whatever had caused the calf's wounds certainly wasn't a natural predator.

While many hoped that the NIDS investigation would expose the tales of the extraordinary events of Skinwalker Ranch as some kind of hallucination, natural phenomenon, or hoax, the opposite occurred. In their book, *Hunt for the Skinwalker* – the basis for a 2018 documentary – Kelleher and Knapp detailed how the group of scientists tried to find an explanation for the plethora of strange activity, including attributing them to experiments being conducted at the nearby army base. However, they could reach no conclusion. "It's as if some cosmic puppet master had written a laundry list of every spooky phenomenon of modern times," said Knapp, "and then unleashed them all in a single location, resulting in a supernatural smorgasbord that no one could possibly believe, much less understand."[11] NIDS disbanded in 2004 after paranormal phenomena at the ranch dramatically decreased.

In 2016, Robert Bigelow sold Skinwalker Ranch to Adamantium Real Estate – a shell corporation of unknown origin – for $4.5 million. All roads leading to the ranch were subsequently blocked and the perimeter guarded by cameras and barbed wire to prevent would-be paranormal investigators from breaking in. "Anyone expecting to find the ranch and see UFOs or Bigfoot will be deeply disappointed," said Knapp in a 2002 article for the *Las Vegas Mercury News*. "Paranormal activity on the property has all but disappeared over the past year, which is a primary reason that access was obtained from NIDS for this article."

In 2017, the *New York Times* broke a story on a secretive government UFO programme named the Advanced Aerospace Weapons Systems Application Program, which had been run by Pentagon counter-intelligence staffer Luis Elizondo. According to the article, in 2007 an unidentified senior official from a national security agency visited Skinwalker Ranch after developing a keen interest in UFOs. According to Knapp, this unidentified individual, whom he described as a "DIA [Defense Intelligence Agency] scientist", had an "experience" while visiting the ranch.[12] That experience made so much of an impression on this individual that he convinced the DIA to seriously investigate paranormal and UFO phenomena. He met with Senator Harry Reid and they decided to start a research program on UFOs. All they needed was somebody with experience in Ufology and paranormal activity to conduct the research.[13] The programme was handed to Bigelow under a government contract, and he received $22 million to study and generate reports on exotic science, UFOs, and other unexplained phenomena. The article added that the bizarre events on Skinwalker Ranch were part of the study, but after two years Bigelow's government funding ran out and the Advanced Aerospace Weapons System Application Program was cancelled. Its findings were never made public and Bigelow remained silent as to what occurred at Skinwalker Ranch.

The *New York Times* piece was accompanied by two videos. The footage showed US Navy jets encountering mysterious craft that were moving at abnormal speeds. The videos went viral and became the subject of fevered speculation by Ufologists. The Navy was forced to confirm the videos' veracity and the dates they were recorded. The footage had been captured by pilots flying from two aircraft carriers, the USS *Nimitz* and the USS *Theodore Roosevelt,* off the coasts of California and Florida in 2004 and 2015. Joseph Gradisher, a spokesman for the office of the Deputy Chief of Naval Operations for Information Warfare, announced that the objects were "unidentified" but said that the Navy would not offer "any hypothesis or conclusions in regard to the objects contained in the referenced videos."[14]

Then in March 2020, Utah-based real-estate mogul Brandon Fugal came forward as the owner of Skinwalker Ranch after remaining anonymous since his 2016 purchase of it. He invited *Vice* magazine to the ranch for a tour and an interview. Fugal had set up the ranch with state-of-the-art sensors and cameras specially designed to detect UFOs and other anomalies. "Skinwalker Ranch, as a project, is so unconventional and so outside of my normal course of business and really, frankly, anyone's normal course of business, that it presents a whole new problem set," Fugal commented. He told *Vice* that, since purchasing Skinwalker Ranch, he had captured evidence of unaccountable injuries, footage of anomalous aerial phenomena, transient EMF, and a number of other mysterious phenomena. He also revealed that extreme electromagnetic fields had been logged on the ranch and detailed that a number of his scientists working at the ranch had become ill – some even required hospitalization. One of them, Thomas Winterton, was hospitalized with fluid on the brain. According to Fugal, this was caused by Winterton attempting to dig on the land. "As for my team, my scientists will be working on releasing reports and information on a peer-reviewed basis in the future," Fugal said.[15] The investigations of Fugal's team were chronicled in a documentary series titled *The Curse of Skinwalker Ranch* on the History channel.

The "living laboratory" that NIDS had created on Skinwalker Ranch represented the largest-ever scientific study of unidentified phenomena in history. Although they were unable to reach a conclusion, many others have attempted to explain what truly happened on Skinwalker Ranch in the late 1990s and early 2000s. Northern Utah is home to a number of army and air force installations, and it has been suggested that military activity could have accounted for the mysterious lights in the sky and UFOs. Some commentators believe that the military was conducting experiments in psychological warfare. However, if that were the case, someone somewhere would have witnessed military men operating in such an isolated and rural area. Ball lightning has also been a theory put forward to explain the strange lights, but according to Terry Sherman, the lights always appeared to be intelligently controlled.

Perhaps not surprisingly, the events at Skinwalker Ranch have been blamed on pranksters, although it is hard to see how a prankster, or a team of pranksters, could be responsible for all of the phenomena witnessed. Some have even simply explained the phenomena away as a case of mass hysteria. However, that explanation does not account for the well-documented cattle mutilations. NIDS themselves even considered the possibility that groups might have been conducting some kind of ritualistic campaign at the ranch. Committed Ufologists have proposed that the phenomena could only be connected to extraterrestrial activity.

Some scientists believe that there is another possibility worth considering: alternate dimensions or parallel universes. According to quantum physics, portals may possibly exist that connect our world to other worlds and alternate dimensions. Based on these theories, it is possible that, hidden on Skinwalker Ranch, is a portal to an unknown world, and that via this portal other entities can come and go.

Skinwalker Ranch has been dubbed "the strangest place on Earth". If the tales surrounding it are to be believed, it certainly appears to have been an epicentre of extraterrestrial activity. "You know, facing the reality of our mortality is sobering. The anomalies at Skinwalker Ranch, the things that have been reported there over decades, if not hundreds, of years seem to attest to the fact that we live in a strange universe," said Brandon Fugal in March 2020. "Perhaps, we're not alone . . ."

The Phoenix Lights

On 13 March 1997, thousands of people in Arizona and Nevada observed strange lights streaking across the sky. These mysterious and unexplainable phenomena have become part of local lore and secured a celebrated place in Ufologist circles as the Phoenix Lights.

"It was definitely not an airplane . . .

I think it was from another world . . .

It was enormous . . ."

Arizona Governor Fife Symington

The Phoenix Lights

The first sighting of what became known as the Phoenix Lights was reported in Henderson, Nevada. At 7:55 pm, an anonymous man reported seeing a V-shaped object in the sky that he estimated to be around the same size as a Boeing 747. He described this object as having six lights along its edges. It was surprisingly quiet; he compared the sound it made to that of a "rushing wind".[1] The V-shaped craft was travelling in a southeasterly direction and disappeared at high speed over the horizon.

The next report came in at around 8:15 pm from Dennis Monroe, a former police officer who lived in the small town of Paulden, Arizona, around 97 km (60 miles) north of Phoenix. He was driving north when he spotted five reddish or orange lights in the sky, heading south. It appeared as though four of the lights were together, while the fifth appeared to be trailing them, or, in his own words, "standing back from the others". The lights were in a V formation, and Monroe estimated that the entire formation covered a part of the sky around the size of his fist held out at arm's length. Staring at the lights through binoculars, he noticed that each one looked as though it was actually made up of two light sources. The lights disappeared over the southern horizon at approximately the same speed as that of a helicopter. "As a police officer, I learned to control my emotions, but this got me pretty excited," said Monroe.[2]

Just minutes later, calls started pouring into the National UFO Reporting Center from citizens of Prescott and Prescott Valley, 24 km (15 miles) south of Paulden. A number of people reported seeing four or five bright lights pass overhead. They could tell that the lights were attached to a UFO because its solid shape had blocked out stars in the sky as it passed overhead. The callers all confirmed that the UFO appeared triangular in shape. One eyewitness, John Kaiser, said that he was outside with his wife and sons when he spotted lights in the sky that formed a triangular pattern. The lights were red, except for the front light, which was a bright white. Another observer said that the lights were definitely white, but that they appeared to change colour.[3] Each person who spotted the UFO asserted that it made no sound, as if it was gliding.

The next sighting came from Dewey, Arizona, around 16 km (10 miles) south of Prescott. A group of five adults and one youth was driving along Highway 69 when they noticed a cluster of lights in the sky in a V shape. They pulled into a grocery store parking lot and clambered out to get a better look. The UFO was directly above them and appeared to hover for several minutes. The anonymous driver estimated that it could not have been more than 1,000 feet (305 m) up; like the earlier witnesses, he noticed that it was eerily silent. This witness reported the sighting to both Prescott Airport and Luke Air Force Base and was told that they had already received numerous sightings of the unidentified object. However, Luke Air Force Base would subsequently claim that it had received no UFO reports from the public.

Reports then flooded in from other Arizona locations – Chino Valley, Wickenburg, Tempe, Glendale, Phoenix, Kingman, and

Tucson. At 8:28 pm, Terry Proctor in Scottsdale videoed the strange lights from 56th St and Carefree Hwy. The tape lasted 42 seconds and showed five small lights in a V formation.

Arizona Governor Fife Symington – a former US Air Force pilot – saw the lights around Phoenix and later described what he saw on the popular CNN television talk show *Larry King Live*: "I saw a craft . . . this large, sort of delta-shaped, wedge-shaped craft moving silently over the valley, over Squaw Peak, dramatically large, very distinctive leading edge with some enormous lights. And it just went on down to the Southeast Valley . . . It was definitely not an airplane . . . I think it was from another world . . . It was enormous . . . the lights over Phoenix was a very compelling, dramatic event seen by so many people that you can't just blow that off and say everybody in Phoenix was hallucinating."

At around 8:20 pm, real-estate consultant Max Saracen and his wife, Shahla, saw a large, black, triangular object pass low overhead. They estimated that its wingspan was vast, over 10,000 feet (3,048 m). "It was a solid mass of metal, but we saw no structure. It blocked the stars out. My wife saw some humanoid shapes at some of its windows. The movie *Independence Day* went through my mind. It was very spooky, this gigantic ship blocking out the stars and silently creeping across the sky. Without a doubt, we believe it was extraterrestrial, from another world."

Shortly afterwards, Tim Ley and his family observed what they described as a large, silent, slow- moving craft in northern Phoenix. Ley said that it was V-shaped and estimated that it had a wingspan of some 1,500 feet (457 m).[4] Nearby, witnesses driving along Interstate 10 described the UFO as blue-grey in colour and said that it took around two minutes to pass over their car.[5]

Truck driver Bill Greiner spotted bright lights while transporting a load of cement down a mountain just north of Phoenix. "Before this, if anybody'd told me they saw a UFO, I would've said, 'Yeah, and I believe in the tooth fairy,'" he said. "I may be just a dumb truck driver but I've seen something that don't belong here."[6] When Greiner spotted the lights, he was within a mile of Luke Air Force Base. He was adamant that, in addition to the lights, he saw three F-16s take off and veer towards the lights. However, when the aircraft came close to the lights, they shot straight up and disappeared "like a blink of an eye".

Many witnesses of the Phoenix Lights preferred to remain anonymous, perhaps fearing ridicule or wishing to avoid publicity. A young man in Phoenix who simply referred to himself as an amateur astronomer spotted the lights as they passed to the west of his home. He described them as solid and unblinking and attached to a UFO. He also said that each light was in fact two smaller lights. Two normal aircraft were flying nearby, one of which turned away from the UFO towards the west, while the other turned away towards the east.

A woman in Phoenix described an object hovering above her house for around five minutes. The UFO then began to slowly move towards the south and appeared to fire a red beam of light from its bow before disappearing out of sight.

A Tucson resident informed the National UFO Reporting Center that he had watched a cluster of lights in the sky for 15 minutes from 8:45 to 9 pm. He said that they had come from the northwest and hovered in the sky, before moving south in a "nose-to-tail" formation before disappearing behind a mountain.

A few kilometres away, Mitch Stanley saw the lights and aimed his 25.4-cm (10-in) telescope at them. He discerned that each light was actually two lights on an aircraft with square wings. "They were planes. There's no way I could have mistaken that," he later told the *Arizona Republic* newspaper. At around 10 pm that night, lights were also spotted over the Gila River and then back over southern Phoenix. 20 minutes later, a retired airline pilot and several others watched as different circular objects flew over Scottsdale Road, Phoenix. According to one of these witnesses, a retired US marshal, the city's lights reflected off the UFO's underside as it flew overhead, blocking out the stars.

In fact, thousands of people saw the lights between 7:55 and 10:30 pm as they passed over a 480-km (300-mile) corridor from the Nevada state line through Phoenix, Arizona, to the northern edge of Tucson, before heading back towards Phoenix. The majority of the reports mentioned a triangular or V-shaped object with linear or diamond-shaped lights along its sides. Some eyewitnesses described two lights on each side with one trailing behind, whereas others described three lights on each side with one trailing behind. Witnesses were divided as to whether the lights were from some kind of large aircraft or independent entities. Those who believed that the lights were on some kind of large craft came to this conclusion because they noticed that its shape blotted out stars as it moved across the night sky. Others, however, said that stars could be seen twinkling *between* the lights. Most witnesses described the lights as being white, but others claimed they were either red, amber, or green; some said the lights where initially white or amber and then changed to red or green.

Differences of opinion in witnesses' accounts led to speculation that people could have seen two completely different objects in the sky. Dr Lynne D. Kitei, a witness to the Phoenix Lights, spent 12 years investigating the events of that night. In her 2004 book *Phoenix Lights: A Skeptic's Discovery That We Are Not Alone*, she concluded that there could have been up to 10 different UFOs. "Whether it was one craft that could morph or a parade of different crafts, we may never know."[7]

Four months after the sightings, the Arizona Air National Guard issued a statement claiming that the mysterious lights were simply flares dropped during a Maryland Air National Guard training exercise. It was standard procedure for military planes to release unused flares before landing. The Public Affairs Office at Luke Air Force Base also announced that they had investigated the Phoenix Lights and established that they were flares that had been launched from eight A-10 jets that had been flying over the Gila Bend Bombing Range, located around 96 km (60 miles) southwest of Phoenix. They claimed that the jets had dropped high-intensity flares from 15,000 feet (4,572 m) to illuminate the target area; the flares fell slowly on parachutes and illuminated a wide area. The statement read:

"[The aircraft] left Davis-Monthan AFB in Tucson at 8:15 pm and returned at 10:00 pm. They were authorized to use the Goldwater range which is near Gila Bend. After their flare exercise they were returning when they realized they had more flares on board. Base regulations forbid planes from landing with flares so they were jettisoned as the planes approached the base."

Even the biggest UFO sceptics found this explanation difficult to accept, and the Arizona Air National Guard's statement prompted a slew of conspiracy theories. Phoenix City Councilwoman Frances Emma Barwood – who had not seen the lights herself – announced that her office wanted to know more about the sightings. She promptly received more than 700 reports. In addition, she believed that many more who had seen the lights that night did not come forward for fear of being ridiculed. "[The National Guard statement] was an insult to the intelligence of the witnesses," she said. "The message to Arizona citizens was that reporting this was stupid."

When officers at Luke Air Force Base were questioned in the immediate aftermath, they refuted witness reports that jets had been scrambled to intercept the lights. They did confirm that F-16s had been sent from the base that night, but said that it was for routine night training. According to Public Affairs Spokesman Senior Airman Petosky, "I can tell you flat out that there was no intercept that night of any lights formation."[8]

For many people, this official statement raised more questions than it answered: why had the Public Affairs Office not mentioned the dropping of flares in connection with the F-16s? Why had the Arizona Air National Guard waited four months before dismissing the lights as flares? Why, after seeing the furore the lights had created, hadn't the F-16 pilots themselves come forward? Official responses also didn't explain why numerous people had seen the lights in locations other than the Phoenix area, nor did they offer any clarity to those who claimed to have seen an object silently hover overhead. Furthermore, flares drift downwards on parachutes, yet none of the witnesses described the lights as travelling in a downwards trajectory. In 2007, Arizona Governor Fife Symington said that what he observed that night "couldn't have been flares because it was so symmetrical . . ."

However, not everyone was prepared to dismiss the authorities' explanation of the Phoenix Lights. Robert Shaeffer of *Skeptical Inquirer* magazine asserted that the Phoenix Lights resulted from two separate incidents, both connected to a programme named Operation Snowbird. This was a pilot-training programme operated by the Air National Guard out of Davis–Monthan Air Force Base in Tucson, Arizona. Firstly, he claimed that those who believed they had seen a single V-shaped object were mistaken: they had actually seen five A-10 jets flying in formation. These aircraft were part of Operation Snowbird, and they had flown from Tucson to Nellis Air Force Base near Las Vegas several days earlier. Shaeffer suggested that on the night that the lights were seen in the sky, the A-10 jets were returning from Las Vegas to Tucson and were flying under visual flight rules, meaning that they did not need to check in with airports along the route. He claimed that, because the A-10 jets were flying in formation, they were employing unblinking formation lights instead of their usual blinking collision lights.

Secondly, Shaeffer reiterated what the Maryland Air National Guard and the Public Affairs Office at Luke Air Force Base had previously announced: the lights seen in the Phoenix area around 10 pm were flare drops from a set of different A-10 jets from the Maryland Air National Guard that were also operating out of Davis–Monthan Air Force Base.

Shaeffer's attempt to explain away the Phoenix Lights event met with much criticism. All of the eyewitnesses had stated that the lights were completely silent (unlike a jet fighter), and many had described the lights as hovering, as opposed to flying. Moreover, the lights moved at a much higher speed than any conventional aircraft and were unlike those of any known aircraft. "The object apparently covered the distance between Paulden and Prescott, AZ – not less than 30 miles [48 km] – in approximately 1–2 minutes . . . and the lights seen on it were not consistent with any type of strobe lights or navigational lights on any type of known aircraft, either private or commercial," observed Peter Davenport, director of the National UFO Reporting Center.[9] Furthermore, Sky Harbor Air

Traffic Control stated that they had spotted the lights in the sky but that no aircraft had showed up on their radar. On 8 March 2000, three Air National Guard pilots tried to re-enact the Phoenix Lights using flares, but could not replicate the formation. In addition, the flares gave off smoke, but no witnesses reported seeing smoke.

Some commentators wondered whether the Phoenix Lights were some sort of secret military exercise. If so, that would explain why no aircraft showed up on Sky Harbor Air Traffic Control's radar screens. According to Mutual UFO Network field investigator Richard Motzer, "The event might have been a military exercise creating holographic images, which would explain why the description varies so much on the object seen that night." Phoenix City councilwoman Frances Emma Barwood attempted to pry the truth from the government but was rebuffed. "Well, if it was a secret military manoeuvre, flying over the sixth-largest city in the nation was not a particularly bright idea," she said. "If the lights were anything else, from an Iraqi invasion to an extraterrestrial visitor, the government needs to let us know if for no other reason than to prevent our imaginations from running rampant."[10]

In the immediate aftermath of the incident, there was speculation that the lights seen in the sky may have been the Hale-Bopp comet. It was a warm, clear evening and many people – like Mutual UFO Network field investigator Alan Morey – were outside, hoping to observe the comet. However, this theory was refuted because a comet appears virtually stationary, while the lights were seen moving rapidly. In fact, a number of people reported seeing both the comet and strange lights in the sky at the same time. James and Fawn Clements were in Kingman, Arizona, when they saw bright lights to the right of the Hale-Bopp comet at around 8 pm. They wondered if another comet had materialized, and through binoculars they discerned five orbs flying southeast in a V-shaped formation.

Alan Morey, who on that night was hoping to view the Hale-Bopp comet, recalled in 2010: "We were on my patio facing due north at 8:30 pm. We had binoculars and had been watching planes land. We saw a cluster of lights coming from the direction of the [Hale-Bopp] comet and moving independently. Extremely bright lights, pale orange in colour. Through the binoculars we could see five independent objects. We knew they were separate because we could see stars between them. They were in a delta-wing configuration headed south. The whole array went over my home. We could hear nothing as they disappeared over South Mountain. My personal view is that it was a military stealth exercise from Nellis Air Force Base in Nevada or Holloman Air Force Base in California."

Perhaps coincidentally, the Northrop Grumman B-2 Spirit, a V-shaped stealth bomber with a wingspan of more than 52 m (170 ft), came into service with the US Air Force in 1997. The question remains whether the military would risk a training exercise so close to Phoenix's three busy airports – Deer Valley, Goodyear, and Sky Harbor – unless it was to test the stealth bomber's ability to evade traditional radar detection.

One of the most prevalent explanations for the Phoenix Lights, in Ufologist circles at least, is that they were a UFO invading US airspace. Some believe that a single UFO was involved; others are adamant that there were multiple UFOs, accounting for the variety of craft and light descriptions. In addition – a recurring meme of reported UFO sightings – some Ufologists maintain that the event was covered up by the authorities.

Accusations of a cover-up stem from the mixed messages that emanated from Luke Air Force Base at the time of the sightings.

The National UFO Reporting Center subsequently received a phone call from an unidentified young man who claimed to be an airman stationed at Luke Air Force Base. He reported that two USAF F-15C fighters had been scrambled to intercept a large triangular object flying at 18,000 feet (5,486 m) over Phoenix. He claimed that they had photographed the UFO with gun cameras before returning to Luke Air Force Base. Two days later, the airman called back to say that his commander had informed him that he was being transferred to an assignment in Greenland, and the Center never heard from him again. The National UFO Reporting Center added that despite the extensive knowledge the caller seemingly had, they were unable to corroborate his claims and were never able to identify him.

Then in January 2009, a witness who identified himself only as "AL" posted on the AboveTopSecret online forum. AL claimed to have first-hand knowledge of how the US Air Force had responded to the Phoenix Lights incident. He wrote: "USAF personnel stationed at both Luke AFB in Glendale and Davis-Monthan AFB in Tucson were a bit scared, as something was occurring over the skies of central and southern Arizona that night, and the on-duty personnel at both bases had no idea what it was." He claimed that Luke Air Force Base scrambled two F-16Cs from the 56th Fighter Wing and sent them in the direction of Tucson, armed with two AIM-9M Sidewinder Missiles and 2-mm Vulcan Cannons. Around ten minutes later, another set of F-16Cs was scrambled, with two additional AIM-7M Sparrow missiles. The anonymous writer claimed that pilots from the first group reported on radio that "something odd" was going on and that they had picked up a radar contact a few thousand feet below and several miles ahead of their position. Their radar showed "clutter", indicative of long-distance, stand-off jamming. He claimed that they then managed to regain radar contact and picked up something large and low "that was beginning to accelerate rapidly". They then lost radar contact with the UFO around 11 km (7 miles) south of Tucson and were ordered to proceed close to the state border and attempt to regain contact. After losing contact, the second group of jets was ordered back to Luke Air Force Base, and around ten minutes later the first jets were ordered back as well.

AL claimed that all of this unfolded while the lights were being spotted in the sky southwest of Phoenix and put forward the theory that the Air Force had dropped flares as a "deception measure" to distract potential observers from focusing on unexplainable phenomena. "Flares were never used that far north of the Goldwater training range ... If they were, there would be weekly Phoenix Lights incidents," he wrote.[11] This distraction theory had already been widely circulated. On the night of the Phoenix Lights, an America West 757 airliner heading to Las Vegas noticed strange lights just north of Phoenix. The three pilots asked the regional air-traffic control centre in Albuquerque what the lights were. A controller radioed back to say that the lights were a flight of CT-144s at 19,000 feet (5,791 m). Overhearing this exchange, a pilot claiming to be part of the formation radioed back: "We're Canadian Snowbirds flying tutors. We're headed to Davis–Monthan Air Force Base." The America West crew was perplexed – why were they flying in show formation at night with their landing lights on and pointed downwards? The 757 pilots said it appeared as though the Canadian Snowbirds were trying to draw attention to themselves for some reason.

The Phoenix Lights event remains the largest-ever mass UFO sighting, cementing Arizona's place in UFO folklore. According to UFO paranormal researcher and author Tom Dongo, "The result of the Phoenix Lights was that it opened a lot of people's minds to the possibility of UFOs."

In 2007, 2008, and 2011, the Phoenix Lights allegedly reappeared, placing Phoenix in the top rank of cities with the most recorded UFO sightings.[12] In 2007, the USAF declared, once again, that the lights seen were flares dropped during F-16 training at Luke Air Force Base; and in 2008, the lights were allegedly caused by a man attaching flares to helium balloons. The 2011 sighting has been attributed to a team of night-time skydivers named the Arizona Skyhawks performing at an event named the Halloween Balloon Spooktacular by jumping out of their plane while carrying flares.

Despite the fact that numerous books, documentaries, radio shows, and even movies have tried to explain the Phoenix Lights, they remain an enigma – and one that had unexpected, tragic consequences. Just 13 days after the reported sightings, 39 members of the Heaven's Gate UFO cult committed suicide. They were convinced that trailing the Hale-Bopp comet was a UFO that would carry them all to a better world.

Picture Credits

The publisher would like to thank the following for their kind permission to reproduce their photographs:

(Key: a-above; b-below/bottom; c-centre; f-far; l-left; r-right; t-top)

Insert 1 Alamy Stock Photo: Granger Historical Picture Archive (tr, cb); Science History Images (tl); M. Timothy O'Keefe (bl). **Insert 2 Alamy Stock Photo:** Abbus Archive Images (bl); The History Collection (tl); Chronicle (crb). **Getty Images:** Dea Picture Library / Contributor (cla). **Insert 3 Alamy Stock Photo:** Landmark Media (bl); Paul Williams (tr); Niday Picture Library (c). **Insert 4 Alamy Stock Photo:** Everett Collection Historical (tl); John Frost Newspapers (tr); Glasshouse Images (cla); Science History Images (clb, br). **Insert 5 Alamy Stock Photo:** CrackerClips Stock Media (cr); Science History Images (cl). **Getty Images:** Joshua Roberts / AFP (t); Ted Soqui / Contributor (b). **Insert 6 Getty Images:** Stuart Deacon / 500px (t). **Insert 7 Alamy Stock Photo:** Everett Collection Inc (tr); TCD / Prod.DB (tl, cra, cb, bl). **Insert 8 Alamy Stock Photo:** Charles Walker Collection (tl, clb); Chronicle (tr); World History Archive (crb). **Insert 9 Alamy Stock Photo:** Chronicle (t, clb). **U.S. Air Force:** Ken LaRock (b). **Insert 10 BBC Photo Library:** Anna Doble (tl). **Dreamstime.com:** Pavel Demin (b). **Insert 11 Alamy Stock Photo:**

American Photo Archive (tc); Granger Historical Picture Archive (ca). **Getty Images:** Bettmann / Contributor (crb). **Rex by Shutterstock:** Anonymous / AP / Shutterstock (bl). **Insert 12 Alamy Stock Photo:** Trinity Mirror / Mirrorpix (cr). **Getty Images:** Daily Mirror / Mirrorpix / Contributor (cl, b). **TopFoto.co.uk:** (tl). **Insert 13 Getty Images:** Terry Fincher / Dtringer / Daily Express / Hulton Archive. **Insert 14 Alamy Stock Photo:** Sean Clarkson (bl); Clynt Garnham Suffolk (tc); Clynt Garnham (c). **Insert 15 Alamy Stock Photo:** © DeepStudios / courtesy Everett Collection (bl); Danita Delimont (t); Witold Skrypczak (cr). **Insert 16 Alamy Stock Photo:** Peter Brogden (clb). **Getty Images:** Education Images / Universal Images Group (t).

Cover images: *Front:* **Nordic Forest by Martin Öhlander;** *Back:* **Emily G.Thompson:** cb

All other images © Dorling Kindersley
For further information see: www.dkimages.com

Endnotes

The Lost Colony of Roanoke

1 *The Virginian-Pilot*, 29 July 2018: "A Lost Colony, An Impossible Mystery"

2 *News & Record*, 11 November 2007: "Our Great Mystery"

3 *The Light and the Glory: 1492 and 1793*, Peter Marshall and David Manuel

4 *The Lost Colony of Roanoke: New Perspectives*, Brandon Fullam

5 *The Historie of Travaile into Virginia Britannia*, William Strachey

6 *Richard Grenville and the Lost Colony of Roanoke*, Any Gabriel-Powell

7 *The News & Observer*, 3 May 2012: "Past Times: Lost Colony Mystery Continues"

8 *Newsmax*, 5 July 2018: "Scientists Seek to Verify Authenticity of Dismissed Roanoke Stone"

9 *Akron Beacon Journal*, 24 April 1998: "Tree Rings Show Severe Drought Ravaged First American Colonies"

10 *The Virginian-Pilot*, 14 April 2017: "Looking for Lost Colony Settlers in All the Wrong Places?"

11 *Winston-Salem Journal*, 17 July 2016: "Artifacts Possibly from Lost Colony Found in Bertie County"

12 *International Business Times*, 15 August 2015: "Secret Club on 400-Year-Old Map May Solve Mystery of Lost Colony of Roanoke"

13 *News & Record*, 8 July 2017: "Lost Colony Settlers May Have Lived with Natives"

14 *The New York Observer*, 10 April 2017: "Debate Over a Gold Ring Revises the Lost Colony of Roanoke Mystery"

15 *International Business Times*, 15 August 2015: "Secret Club on 400-Year-Old Map May Solve Mystery of Lost Colony of Roanoke"

16 *The Virginian-Pilot*, 31 March 2001: "New Hints to Lost Colonists Found Settlers May Have Gone West with the Croatan Indian People"

17 *Yes Weekly*, 6 June 2018: "Secret Token Examines White America's Fascination with the Lost Colony"

18 *A New Voyage to Carolina*, John Lawson

The Mystery of the *Mary Celeste*

1 *Mary Celeste: The Greatest Mystery of the Sea*, Paul Begg

2 *Mary Celeste: The Greatest Mystery of the Sea*, Paul Begg

3 *Lost at Sea: The Truth Behind Eight of History's Most Mysterious Ship Disasters*, A. Hoehling

4 *Quad-City Times*, 20 December 1965: "What Happened to the Ship Mary Celeste?"

5 *Pembroke Daily Observer*, 30 July 2015: "No Human Ingenuity Can Account for the Abandonment"

6 *Smithsonian*, 1 November 2007: "Abandoned Ship – What Really Happened Aboard the *Mary Celeste*?"

7 *The Daily Herald-Tribune*, 12 October 2001: "Maritime Mystery Solved"

8 *The Toronto Star*, 23 July 1989: "Why Was the *Mary Celeste* Abandoned?"

9 *Ghost Ship: The Mysterious True Story of the* Mary Celeste *and Her Missing Crew,* Brian Hicks

10 *The Indianapolis News,* 28 February 1873: "Bad News"

11 *Brooklyn Daily Eagle,* 9 March 1902: "Mystery of Lost Crew of the *Mary Celeste*"

12 *Arizona Republic,* 7 February 1943: "Son's Greatest Mystery Has Never Been Solved"

The Flannan Lighthouse Mystery

1 *The Sunday Mail,* 13 October 2019: "Greed, Insanity, Murder, or Swept to their Deaths in a Winter Storm?"

2 *The Guardian,* 29 December 1900: "Disaster at Lewis Lighthouse"

3 *The Times,* 26 December 1990: "Boxing Day at Flannan Rock – Life and Times"

4 *The Age,* 21 September 1935: "Mysteries of the Sea"

5 *The Scariest Places in the World,* Bob Curran

6 *The Scariest Places in the World,* Bob Curran

7 *The Atlanta Constitution,* 16 December 1979: "The Random Time Machine"

8 *McX: Scottish X Files,* Ron Halliday

9 *The Sunday Herald,* 20 June 2010: "Mystery Writers Retreat to Scotland's Creepiest Island"

10 *Tock Lighthouses of Britain: The End of an Era?,* Christopher P. Nicholson

11 *Albert Jack's Ten-Minute Mysteries,* Albert Jack

12 *The Sunday Mirror,* 2 December 1999: "Riddle of Lighthouse Keepers Who Vanished From Island"

13 *The Express,* 9 October 2015: "Lighthouse Riddle Solved?"

14 *The Scotsman,* 22 August 2000: "Sea Trip Marks Centenary of Isles' Unsolved Mystery"

The Disappearance of Amelia Earhart

1 *St Louis Post-Dispatch*, 13 July 2003: "Atchison's Amelia Earhart Festival Celebrates a Pioneer of Flight"

2 *Amelia Earhart: Legendary Aviator*, Brenda Haugen

3 *The Wichita Eagle*, 29 September 1991: " 54 Years a Mystery"

4 *Life*, 19 May 1997: "First Lady of the Sky"

5 *Amelia Earhart: The Mystery Solved*, Marie K. Long and Elgen M. Long

6 *The Columbus Dispatch*, 1 July 2007: "Vanished Pioneer – Expedition Soon Might Solve 1937 Mystery of Amelia Earhart"

7 *Amelia Earhart: The Lost Evidence*, History channel

8 *Amelia Earhart: The Truth at Last*, Mike Campbell

9 *International Business Times*, 12 July 2017: "Tokyo-Based Blogger Shuts Claims Amelia Earhart Died a Japanese Captive"

10 *International Business Times*, 30 October 2014 – "Fragments of Lost Lockheed Electra Suggests Pilot Died as Castaway"

11 *International Business Times*, 6 July 2017: "Amelia Earhart Found"

12 *International Business Times*, 9 March 2018: "Bones Found on Western Pacific Ocean Island Likely to Be Amelia Earhart's"

13 The *Washington Post*, 25 July 2018: "Dozens Heard Amelia Earhart's Final, Chilling Pleas for Help, Researchers Say"

14 *The Daily Mirror*, 31 January 2019: "Mysterious Wreck Discovered off Papua New Guinea"

15 www.porjectblueangel.com/about

16 *Eyewitness: The Amelia Earhart Incident*, Thomas E. Devine and Richard M. Daley

17 *USA Today*, 17 March 1992: "The Last Days of Amelia Earhart"

The Roswell Incident

1 *Dallas Morning News*, 22 May 1994 – "Alien Notion – In 1947, Something Crashed in the High Desert Near Roswell, N.M."

2 *Albuquerque Journal*, 6 July 1947 – "Veterans Hospital Patients Report Flying Disc Here"

3 *Crash at Corona: The U.S. Military Retrieval and Cover-up of a UFO* by Don Berliner and Stanton Friedman

4 *Witness to Roswell* by Thomas J. Carey and Donald R. Schmitt

5 *Sun Sentinel*, 29 June 2014 – "Truth Is Out There"

6 *Roswell Daily Record*, 9 July 1947 – "Harassed Rancher Who Located 'Saucer' Sorry He Told About It"

7 *Expose: Roswell UFO Incident*, John Tilley

8 *The Roswell Incident: An Eyewitness Account*, Debbie Schmitt and Thomas J. Carey

9 *True Stories of Space Exploration Conspiracies*, Nick Redfern

10 *Witness to Roswell*, Thomas J. Carey and Donald R. Schmitt

11 *Odessa American*, 3 September 2015: "Questions Still Linger About Roswell"

12 *Kansas City Star*, 25 June 1997: "Space Invaders! Air Force Released Photographs of Dummy 'Aliens' in Another Effort to Dispel Myth of 1947 UFO Crash"

13 *UFOs Today: 70 Years of Lies, Misinformation & Government Cover-up*, Irena Scott

14 *UFOs and the National Security State: Chronology of a Cover-up, 1941–1973*, Richard M. Dolan

15 *UFOs and the National Security State: Chronology of a Cover-up, 1941–1973*, Richard M. Dolan

16 *Dallas Morning News,* 15 January 1995: "N.M. Town Is a Mecca for UFO Buffs – Roswell Is Home to Two Museums"

The Flatwoods Monster

1 *The Monster and the Saucer,* Gray Barker

2 The *Ogden Standard-Examiner,* 14 September 1952: "10-ft Monster Scares Party"

3 The *Miami News,* 15 September 1952: "Story of Monster Arouses Skepticism"

4 The *Augusta Chronicle,* 17 December 2000: "Mysterious Monsters Haunted West Virginia Town"

5 *Skeptical Inquirer,* 2 November 2000: "The Flatwoods UFO Monster"

6 *Princetown Daily Clarion,* 15 September 1952: "Flying Saucer Land; Huge Glowing Monster Approaches Witness"

7 *News-Journal,* 19 September 1952: " 'Metallic Monster' Goes Unexplained"

8 The *Baltimore Sun,* 23 September 1952: "Scientist Quizzes Observers of West Virginia Saucer"

9 *The Braxton County Monster: The Cover-Up of the Flatwoods Monster Revealed,* Frank C. Feschino

10 The *Charleston Daily Mail,* 16 September 1969: "Monster Rite Revisited"

11 *Mothman and Other Curious Encounters,* Loren Coleman

12 *The Baltimore Sun,* 30 October 2002: "Flatwoods Monster Anniversary Marked

13 *Charleston Gazette,* 12 September 2002: "Area Event Celebrating 50 Years: Braxton County Monster"

14 *Charleston Gazette,* 12 October 2004: "Author Follows the Trail of the Braxton County Monster"

15 *Monsters of West Virginia: Mysterious Creatures in the Mountain State,* Visionary Living, Inc.

16 *Dallas Examiner,* 20 March 2011: "1952 UFO Wave and the Flatwoods Monster Mystery"

17 *Associated Press,* 2 November 2019: "The W. Va. Monster that Crept into International Pop Culture"

18 *Charleston Gazette,* 29 April 2015: "County Embraces Monster Folklore"

The Dyatlov Pass Incident

1 *Dead Mountain: The Untold True Story of the Dylatov Pass Incident,* Donnie Eichar

2 *Pembroke Daily Observer,* 8 March 2012, "I Would Ask God What Really Happened to my Friends That Night"

3 Tagil Worker's Newspaper, 18 February 1959 – "Unusual Celestial Phenomenon"

4 *Leninskiy Put,* 24 November 1990 – "Mystery of the Fireballs"

5 *Los Angeles Examiner,* 31 May 2014 – "Bigfoot Expert Weighs in on 'Russian Yeti: The Killer Lives'"

6 Tass, 21 July 2016 – "Dyatlov Pass Mystery Victims Could Have Been on KGB Mission - Researcher

7 *Yerepouni Daily News,* 3 February 2020 – "The Russian Conspiracy Theory That Won't Die"

8 *Death on the Trail*, Alexei Rakitin

9 *The Death of the Hikers*, Gennadit Kozilov

10 Tass, 4 February 2019 – "Prosecution Agencies Rule Out Authorities' Involvement in 1959 Dyatlov Pass Incident"

11 *Pembroke Daily Observer*, 8 March 2012 – "I Would Ask God What Really Happened to my Friends That Night"

The Abduction of Barney and Betty Hill

1 *Captured: The Betty and Barney Hill UFO Experience*, Kathleen Marden and Stanton T. Friedman

2 *The Interrupted Journey: Two Lost Hours Aboard a Flying Saucer*, John G. Fuller

3 *Concord Monitor*, 11 April 2009: "More than Abductees"

4 *The Portsmouth Herald*, 8 February 2016: "History Matters – What Barney Hill Saw in the Night Sky 55 Years After the Incident UFO Debate Persists"

5 *Dallas Examiner*, 18 October 2011: "Strange Facts About UFO History"

6 *The Caledonian-Record*, 17 September 2011: "The Hill File"

7 *Carlsbad Current-Argus*, 1 July 2017: "Roswell UFO Festival – They Do Exist"

8 *The Seattle Times*, 19 October 2004: "Betty Hill, 85, Gained Fame with Alien Abduction Tale"

9 *Wicked Local*, 3 April 2009: "Paranormal Researcher Remembers the Hill Alien Abduction Story"

10 *San Jose Examiner*, 26 July 2011: "Most Famous UFO Story Ever: Betty and Barney Hill Alien Abduction Incident"

11 *Los Angeles Times*, 24 October 2004: "Betty Hill, 85; Claim of Abduction by Aliens Led to Fame"

The Falcon Lake Incident

1 *Winnipeg Free Press* obituaries, 28 July 2015

2 *Winnipeg Free Press* obituaries, 30 October 1999

3 *Winnipeg Free Press,* 20 May 2017: "Burned, Bewildered, and Badgered"

4 CBC, 19 May 2017: "Falcon Lake Incident Is Canada's Best-Documented UFO Case"

5 *My Encounter with the UFO,* Stefan Michalak

6 *Alien Contacts and Abductions,* Jenny Randles

7 *The Falcon Lake Case: Too Close an Encounter,* Chris Rutkowski

8 *Steinbach Carillon,* 26 May 2017: "Truth Is Out There Near Falcon Lake"

9 *Toronto Star,* 13 November 1999: "Opening the U-Files – Everyone Loves to Visit Ontario – Even UFOs"

10 *Winnipeg Free Press,* 25 May 1997: "Unexplained Sighting"

11 *The Toronto Star,* 6 March 2018: "Meet the Man Who Worked on Infamously Nixed Avro Arrow!

12 CBC, 3 April 2018: "Mint's Newest Coin Showcases Famous Falcon Lake Encounter in Manitoba"

13 *The Hamilton Spectator,* 3 April 2018: "Royal Canadian Mint Releases Coin Depicting Manitoba Man's UFO Encounter"

The Isdal Woman

1 *The Express,* 12 August 2018: "50-Year Mystery of Burnt Beauty in the Ice Valley"

2 *The Isdal Woman – Operation Isotopsy: Death in Ice Valley,* Tore Osland

3 *NRK,* 29 November 2016: "The Isdalen Mystery"

4 *The Times*, 20 May 2017: "New Clues Over Burnt Body of Norway Spy"

5 *Die Zeit*, 23 May 2018: "I Saw Her"

6 *NRK*, 28 May 2018: "Father Warned of Possible Spy"

7 *The Woman in the Isdalen*, Dennis Aske

8 *Bergens Tidende*, 10 August 2018: "Who Is the Isdal Woman Case?"

9 *Bergens Tidende*, 21 March 2018: "The Ice Valley Woman Was Not a Prostitute"

10 *NRK*, 23 October 2016: "Threw Gasoline on and Ignited"

11 *NRK*, "Police Acts: 1970"

12 *NRK*, 19 May 2017: "Chemical Analysis of the Isdal Woman Points to Germany and France"

The D. B. Cooper Hijacking

1 *The D. B. Cooper Hijacking: Vanishing Act*, Kay Melchisedech Olson

2 *Toronto Sun*, 28 March 2003: "Moments After Takeoff, D. B. Cooper Handed a Stewardess a Folded Piece of Paper"

3 *The Legend of D. B. Cooper*, Pat Forman and Ron Forman

4 *Danville Register*, 14 November 1976: "Dan Cooper Jumped from Airliner with $200,000 Strapped to His Body Five Years Ago"

5 *Skyjack: The Hunt for D. B. Cooper*, Geoffrey Gray

6 *Mercury News*, 4 August 2011: "My Uncle Was D. B. Cooper"

7 *Chicago Sun-Times*, 9 August 2011: "No Match to D. B. Cooper"

8 *Wichita Eagle*, 1 July 1989: "Legend Grows and Grows, Are Skyjacker, Killer One and Same?"

9 *News-Register*, 24 May 2007: "Sheridan Man Laughs Off D. B. Cooper Talk"

10 *Dedham Transcript,* 26 October 2007: "D. B. Cooper Found?"

11 The Associated Press, 23 November 2007: "36th Anniversary of D. B. Cooper's Skyjacking"

12 *Oregonian,* 10 July 2010: "Robert Rackstraw, D. B. Cooper Suspect with Various Bizarre Oregon Connections, Dies at 75"

13 *Birmingham News,* 29 June 2018: "Is Robert Rackstraw Hijacker D. B. Cooper?"

14 *Oregonian,* 16 July 2018: "Skyjacker Revealed Identity to Oregonian, Code-Breaker Claims"

15 *Bay City Times,* 22 May 2018: "D. B. Cooper Was Michigan Man"

16 *Dallas Morning News,* 20 November 1986: "Search for D. B. Cooper to Be Resumed"

The Lord Lucan Case

1 *A Different Class of Murder: The Story of Lord Lucan,* Laura Thompson

2 *The Salt Lake Tribune,* 17 June 1975: "Wife Tells of Attack by Playboy Peer"

3 *Nanaimo Daily News,* 18 November 1979: "Where Is Mysterious Lord Lucan?"

4 *A Different Class of Murder: The Story of Lord Lucan,* Laura Thompson

5 *The Tampa Tribune,* 17 June 1975: "Lady Lucan Tells of Strangling"

6 *A Different Class of Murder: The Story of Lord Lucan,* Laura Thompson

7 *The Galveston Daily News,* 26 October 1978: "Gambling Earl Takes a Chance, But May Lose Everything"

8 *International Business Times*, 23 July 2016: "Lord Lucan Was Killed 'Mafia Style'
in Switzerland by His Rich Friends, Claims Novelist"

9 *International Business Times*, 30 January 2016: "Lord Lucan Was 'Fed to Tiger' After He Shot Himself"

10 *The Observer*, 19 February 2012: "Lucan Children and the 'Secret Trips to Africa'"

11 *The Scotsman*, 16 June 2014: "Lord Lucan Fled to Greece with ex-MI5 Agents' Help"

12 *Looking for Lucan*, Roy Ranson and Robert Strange

13 *I News*, 29 January 2020: "Lord Lucan: The Claim the Aristocrat Is Alive and Buddhist in Australia Is the Most Recent in a Long Line of Spottings"

14 *BBC News*, 10 January 2018: "Lady Lucan Died After Taking 'Cocktail of Drink and Drugs'"

15 *The Independent*, 19 September 1998: "Lord Lucan, I Presume?"

16 *The Telegraph*, 18 January 2018: "Lady Lucan Cut Her Children Out of Her Will Because of 'Lack of Good Manners,' Probate Document Reveals"

The Rendlesham Forest Incident

1 *A Covert Agenda: The British Government's UFO Top Secrets Exposed*, Nick Redfern

2 RAF Memo, Lieutenant Colonel Charles I. Halt

3 *UFOs: Generals, Pilots, and Government Officials Go on the Record*, Leslie Kean

4 "New Light on Rendlesham," Dr David Clarke: drdavidclarke. co.uk/secret-files/secret-files-4

5 *The UFO Files: The Inside Story of Real-Life Sightings,* David Clarke

6 *You Can't Tell the People,* Georgina Bruni and Nick Pope

7 The Halt Tapes: www.ianridpath.com/ufo/halttape.htm

8 *The Daily Telegraph,* 31 December 2018: "Britain's Roswell: What Really Happened in the Rendlesham Forest UFO Incident?"

9 *The People,* 23 September 2012: "The Rendlesham Forest Incident"

10 "The 3AM Fireball – How It All Started," Ian Ridpath: www.ianridpath.com/ufo/rendlesham1d.htm

11 *UFO Crash Landing? Friend or Foe?,* Jenny Randles

12 *UFOS and Nukes: The Secret Link Revealed,* 2016

13 *UFO FAQ: All That's Left to Know About Roswell, Aliens, Whirling Discs, and Flying Saucers,* David J. Hogan

14 *East Anglian Daily Times,* 6 January 2017: "Book Promises 'Truth' About UFO Mystery"

15 *East Anglian Daily Times,* 2 January 2019: "Rendlesham Forest UFO 'Was SAS Pranking the Americans'?"

16 *East Anglian Daily Times,* 7 September 2018: "We Are Not Alone – UFO-Spotting Colonel Halt Shares His Memories"

Skinwalker Ranch

1 *The Daily Beast,* 2 July 2015: "Why Do UFOs Love This Utah Ranch So Much?"

2 *Hunt for the Skinwalker,* Colm Kelleher and George Knapp

3 *Uintah Basin Standard,* 24 September 2016: "Skinwalker Ranch Activity Shifts from Paranormal to Prosecutable"

4 *Deseret News,* 30 June 1996: "Frequent Fliers?"

5 *Salt Lake City Examiner,* 3 May 2010: "Utah's Skinwalker Ranch"

6 *The Path of the Skinwalker*, George Knapp

7 *Seeking Out the Skinwalker*, April Slaughter

8 *Las Vegas Review-Journal*, 3 December 2005: "Knapp Shows Guts by Treading on Shaky Ground of UFO Sightings"

9 *Santa Fe New Mexican*, 24 October 1996: "Millionaire Buys Utah's 'UFO Ranch'"

10 *Deseret News*, 22 April 2006: "Mysteries of 'UFO Ranch' in Spotlight"

11 *Las Vegas CityLife*, 2 February 2006: "The Truth Could Be in There"

12 UFO MegaCon, 2019

13 *New York Times*, 16 December 2017: "Glowing Auras and Black Money"

14 *Air & Space*, 1 February 2020: "In 2019, Our Eyes Were on the Skies"

15 *Vice*, 10 March 2020: "This Is the Real Estate Magnate Who Bought Skinwalker Ranch, a UFO Hotspot"

The Phoenix Lights

1 Summary of Phoenix Lights Event by Peter B. Davenport: http://www.ufoevidence.org/documents/doc1276.htm

2 *Life Examiner*, 24 February 2010: "Were the 1997 Arizona Lights a Psychological Warfare Experiment?"

3 National UFO Reporting Center News Release, 13 March 1997: "UFO Events Over Arizona"

4 *Phoenix Examiner*, 1 May 2010: "National Geographic Phoenix Lights Investigation Provokes New Phoenix Lights UFO Witness Report"

5 *A World of UFOs*, Chris A. Rutowski

6 *Baxter Bulletin,* 18 June 1997: "UFO Reports Stir Up Phoenix"

7 *Phoenix Magazine,* 1 March 2017: "Q & A With Dr Lynne Kitei on 20th Anniversary of Phoenix Lights"

8 *Life Examiner,* 28 February 2010: "Were the 1997 Arizona Lights a Psychological Warfare Experiment?"

9 *A World of UFOs,* Chris A. Rutowski

10 *The Augusta Chronicle,* 6 September 1998: "Politician Wants Truth About Phoenix Lights"

11 http://www.abovetopsecret.com/forum/thread429061/pg1

12 *The Scottsdale Times,* 1 March 2012: "Out Of This World"